WITHDRAWN

Dance-Based Dance Theory

NEW STUDIES IN AESTHETICS

Robert Ginsberg
General Editor

Vol. 7

PETER LANG
New York · San Francisco · Bern
Frankfurt am Main · Paris · London

GV
1588.3
.A45
1991

Judith B. Alter

Dance-Based Dance Theory

From Borrowed Models
to Dance-Based Experience

OC # - 22734427

mNGA

PETER LANG
New York · San Francisco · Bern
Frankfurt am Main · Paris · London

Library of Congress Cataloging-in-Publication Data

Alter, Judith B.
    Dance-based dance theory : from borrowed
models to dance-based experience / Judith B. Alter.
        p. cm. — (New studies in aesthetics ; vol. 7)
    Includes bibliographical references and index.
    1. Dancing—Philosophy.   I. Title.   II. Series.
GV1588.3.A45   1991   792.6′2—dc20   90-23458
ISBN 0-8204-1532-4   CIP
ISSN 0893-6005

© Peter Lang Publishing, 1991

All rights reserved.
Reprint or reproduction, even partially, in all forms such as
microfilm, xerography, microfiche, microcard, offset strictly
prohibited.

Printed in the United States of America.

TABLE OF CONTENTS

PREFACE

This book about dance theory is written for dance scholars, aestheticians, and readers interested in dance. It offers a revised research paradigm for dance, an inductive method for evaluating dance theoretical writing, and a critical analysis of the writing on dance by eighteen thinkers. It contains the first in-depth study of the ideas of Elizabeth Selden, John Martin, and Margaret H'Doubler. It critically presents the ideas about dance of thirteen influential aestheticians who wrote at the same time as Susanne K. Langer. And it suggests that the ideas, methods, and theories of Rudolf Laban provide a model for dance researchers, thereby enabling us to separate from philosophy and declare autonomy as a dance-based independent field.

This book grew through three stages. The first occurred at Harvard Graduate School of Education in 1978 when philosophy professor Vernon Howard wrote, "This has the seeds of a dissertation" on the margin of my first paper. I had analyzed Collingwood's ideas about dance, and to explain how thorough was his understanding I used parallel ideas from John Martin's book *Introduction to the Dance*. The juxtaposition of these books revealed that the structure of Martin's book paralleled Collingwood's. During a discussion of this paper with Jeanne Beaman (my dance advisor outside Harvard), I identified the pattern of twentieth-century dance writers borrowing theoretical concepts from philosophers. Like most of my contemporaries, I had been taught that only Langer had written about dance as an art; therefore I was surprised to find in the philosophy section of Widener Library more than a dozen other twentieth century aestheticians who wrote about dance as an art. When I analyzed the ideas about dance by these aestheticians, I learned that their primary sources about dance were books of dance theory.

My research in the field of dance theory grew into a dissertation under the guidance of Vernon Howard. I am grateful to him and to Jeanne Beaman, Gertrude Lippincott, Israel Scheffler and Daniel Pekarsky for wisely advising, assisting, and informing me during my Harvard work.

The next stage of this research occurred while I taught this material to undergraduate and graduate classes at the University of Wisconsin, Madison, and the University of California, Los Angeles. At the University of California, Riverside, in the intercampus Dance History Masters Degree Program, I tested the basic pattern in centuries preceding the twentieth century as I taught the History of Dance Theory. To those many students who challenged and deepened these ideas I am very appreciative.

Three years ago I re-examined the material with a fresh attitude challenging myself to bring it to maturity. Studying and analyzing the writings of Laban reassured me that deriving dance-based research methods, concepts, and theory was a realizable goal. I am grateful to Naima Prevots, Malcolm Nicol, Christina Schlundt, Ruth Hapgood, my editor at Houghton Mifflin, and Judy Scalin for their suggestions and help at this stage. I appreciate the suggestions on the Laban chapter from Vera Maletic and Judy Gantz. I also am grateful to Peter Bassett, Senior Librarian at the Laban Centre for Movement and Dance, for his help in finding lost references, and to William Roberts, Archivist at the University of California, Berkeley, for his help in finding biographic information about Elizabeth Selden. (No one has found a recorded date of her death.)

When Robert Ginsberg, editor of New Studies in Aesthetics, accepted and edited the book for Peter Lang Publishing, I revised my manuscript on a new level and began working with a professional editor, Randy Woodland, a faculty member in the Writing Programs at UCLA. Randy would say, quietly, "Tell me about this idea." I would, and he would then say, "Good, now write that here!" Under his expert and patient guidance, I sharpened the sentences, paragraphs, and chapters, and eventually reshaped the entire book. After choreographing dances for twenty-two years, I began to learn how to choreograph words.

I appreciate permission to reprint the following: Margaret H'Doubler's diagrams granted by the University of Wisconsin Press; Laban's "Alphabet of Basic Symbols of Labanotation" granted by Dance Notation Bureau; and a page of Labanotation research on the *cinque passi* step of the galliard by Maria Drabecka in *Dance Studies*, Volume 1, 1976, edited by Roderyk Lange. The Labanotated dance is from my Master's Thesis Concert Notebook, 1970, Mills College, Oakland, California. An earlier version of the chapter on Collingwood appeared in *New Dimensions in Dance*, edited by Diana T. Taplin, Pergamon Press, 1979, and an earlier version of the chapter on Langer appeared in *CORD Annual 1983-84*. I made the drawings for the book to add visual dance ideas to the written ones.

Dance-Based Dance Theory examines the problems and issues in writing about the physical, kinesthetic, visual and aural experience of dance. I combined the ethnologist's method of making the familiar strange with the role of a participant observer to uncover the many strengths and weaknesses in the writing of the aestheticians and dance theorists analyzed here. Therefore personal knowledge became one of my criteria for judging the accuracy, completeness, and ultimately the value of the writings about dance. I invite my readers to join me in this process of rediscovery.

Los Angeles, California
July, 1990

1
TOWARD AUTONOMY

At the turn of this century, the revolution in theater dance radically influenced the academic progress of dance when a significant number of dance practitioners rejected ballet as the main theatrical form and inventively developed new forms which became known as "modern dance." During the same period, dance became a creative outlet used in pageants popular all over America and Europe. American college courses in pageantry included instruction in "creative" dance.[1]   Though dance classes were offered in private high schools, academies, and colleges in the 1800s, a dance major was not established until 1927. By the end of the 1920s, creative dance was recognized by educators as sufficiently rigorous and autonomous a subject to offer as a major. Today more than 250 dance departments and dance majors exist in American colleges and universities, yet only in the past twenty years has a doctorate been available in dance. The changes in the profession and in the academic status of dance at educational institutions stimulated dance scholars, teachers, and critics to write theoretical books about dance as an autonomous field of study.

Only in the twentieth century has the academic study of dance separated from music and drama. This emerging autonomy together with outside factors has stimulated growth in dance scholarship. The academic recognition of dance as a scholarly discipline brought the consequent need for adequate dance literature to study. The availability of masters and doctoral degrees in dance attracted students interested in examining the theoretical issues of dance activity. Their collective interests stimulated the emergence of research-oriented scholarly organizations which hold conferences and produce publications: the Society for Dance History Scholars, Dance Critics Association, Congress on Research in Dance are examples.

The move toward scholarly autonomy in dance was paralleled in many academic disciplines during the early part of this century. At that time, fields such as psychology and anthropology separated from the speculative realm of philosophy, their parent field, to become autonomous and "scientific." In a "scientific" approach, scholars study their subject directly by examining the actual experience they hope to explain instead of only citing what other thinkers have speculated about the subject and then arguing the merits of those "expert" ideas. Some writers on dance are slow to relinquish this referential and deferential style of writing about dance.

This book examines the changes which began early in the twentieth century in the fields of dance and aesthetics. These fields influenced each other; I propose to analyze those influences, thus revealing the insights and limitations of each field. This study weaves together intellectual history of the two fields with textual analysis of books on "dance theory" and of chapters on dance by aestheticians (philosophers who offer philosophical analyses of the arts) written between 1920 and 1976.

The development of dance as an autonomous academic field stimulates the quest for a theoretical base and productive research methods to derive theoretical concepts about the field. Traditionally, dance writers turned to aestheticians to validate their ideas about dance. The reliance on outside experts resulted in many unexamined ideas being carried forward into contemporary dance literature. Dependence on philosophy may have done more harm than good for the theoretical development of dance.

This dependence on aesthetics has a long tradition in Western dance history. In books of European and American dance theory written from the fifteenth century to the present, I find dance writers regularly incorporating into their explanations of dance current ideas about the nature and value of art. When aestheticians defended the arts as rational, dance theorists justified dance as rational. When the aestheticians valued the arts because they stimulated the imagination, dance theorists justified dance in the same way. When aestheticians thought the arts were important for their expressive and communicative powers (the early twentieth-century vogue), dance writers explained the value of dance as expressive of universal feelings communicated to an audience. Western dance writings echo whatever is fashionable in aesthetics.

The variations in aesthetic explanations extend to specific wording and detail, though the contents of the dance theory texts remain focussed on similar dance topics, issues, and goals. John Weaver, in his *An Essay*

Towards an History of Dancing (1712), defends dance as imitative motions used "to explain things conceived in the mind . . . and plainly and intelligibly representing Actions, Manners, and Passions."[2] Weaver's emphasis on the "mind" framing intelligible motions reflects humanism and the value of reason in life and art. Louis de Cahusac, in *La Danse Ancienne et Moderne* (1754), claims dance is valuable because it stimulates the imagination and gives people pleasure.[3] His ideas reflect the anti-rational swing in aesthetics: art is valued because it adds joy and fantasy to life and frees people from boredom. In his *Lettres sur la Danse, et les Ballets* (1760), Jean George Noverre highlights the need for unstylized movement to depict real people in pleasant natural surroundings. This emphasis reflects naturalism, in which arts display reality through instinctive and spontaneous (not intellectual) expression.[4] In his *Traité Élémentaire, Théorique et Pratique de l'Art de la Danse* (1820), Carlo Blasis expounds on grace, naturalism, and pleasure-giving in dancing, reflecting the early romantic value of art which displays charm, play, delight, and beauty.[5]

The shared cultural milieux in which the aestheticians and dance writers worked certainly influenced their commonly held ideas and changing values, and one might argue that the aestheticians reflected dance practices in their writings. A little historical investigation reveals the reverse: the dance theorists write their ideas using the terms of simplified and popular interpretations of aesthetic ideas. Though these ideas reflect the common practice of the times, rarely does either group of writers analyze immediately current art practices, because time and reflection are necessary for identifiable patterns to emerge before aestheticians or dance theorists can analyze them.

The use of philosophic conceptual models and non-dance theoretical explanations of dance by dance theorists causes further problems. Not only do dance writers adjust the content of dance theory to fit the current aesthetic theory, but they use a philosophic approach for writing comprehensive dance theory which is characterized by broad generalizations unsubstantiated by physical examples. When they refer to dances, these writers assume their readers are familiar with a waltz, social dance, or ballet and fail to explain their dance references. The writers compound the problem created by their generalizations by not defining such crucial terms as "movement," a "dance," "center," "impulse," or even "time," "space," and "force."

Popular usage of the word "dance" adds to the confusion in serious writing about it. When high school students go to their "dance," they mean the Prom. The word "dance" in "May I have this dance?" refers to a popular (vernacular, social, ballroom) dance. Attending a "dance" concert implies seeing several separate dances, though going to the "Ballet" may mean seeing a full-length work or three or four short ones. And this book is about the field of "Dance": incorporating all features and functions of dance in personal, cultural, and universal terms. The several meanings of the word "dance" explain why students in non-art majors in college do not understand what there is to study when a fellow student says he or she is majoring in Dance. Writers and readers need to clarify whether "dance" refers to the singular or collective, general or specific, vernacular or academic meaning.

Another characteristic of philosophic writing carried into dance writing is the use of dichotomies to polarize an issue. These dichotomies simplify analysis by focussing on the negative attributes of the two poles or on characteristics they lack. The dichotomies might not reflect the complex concepts embodied in significant words. Dichotomies found throughout theoretical writing about dance are: mind and body, emotion and reason, conscious and unconscious, active and passive, doing and thinking, theory and practice, means and ends, art and craft, subjective and objective. Though serving a useful end in aesthetics, these dichotomies need to be re-examined since they restrict accurate and complex understanding of central issues in the analysis of dance theory and practice.

Borrowed concepts are derived from research methods geared to their particular fields. In their writing about dance for academic purposes, dance scholars have traditionally applied concepts from other disciplines to dance without being fully aware that those research methods may not be applicable to dance at the level of depth the dance writers intend. This borrowing of concepts by dance scholars reverses the order of the steps usually followed in academic research.

Though they employ methods specific to their field, researchers in most fields are primarily guided by the "scientific method," which depends on empirical data, on experience of the senses rather than only on theory.

Empirical research follows this paradigm: question, investigation, conclusion. Questions are usually inductive, often based on a hunch; they center on basic issues about phenomena. Investigation starts with a review of the literature, usually written by scholars in the field or related fields, and then proceeds to the study of real material, events, or phenomena. The study takes place in the laboratory or in the real world, preferably in both. After data are gathered, processed, sorted, analyzed, and considered, researchers draw conclusions. Other researchers then challenge these conclusions with more studies until members of the field are confident of the validity and reliability of the conclusions. Then they trust the conclusions as theoretically sound. Many dance theorists have reversed this process, starting their research process about dance issues and questions by trusting the accuracy of conclusions from other fields.

The review of the literature has been the starting point of much dance research. But dance researchers have turned to literature from fields other than their own, trusting the "truth" of theoretical concepts developed by research in other fields, research guided by implicit criteria about what questions are valuable and how research is evaluated. These ideas are written in discipline-specific language, called jargon. The dance scholars who use theoretical concepts from other fields are unaware of how those methods, goals, and foci could contradict, undermine, or detract from their basic research needs in dance.

The goals and methods of the fields of dance and aesthetics differ. In 1947 aesthetician Harry B. Lee explained: the aim of the aesthetician "is to construct a better theory of the universe than his predecessor; he is not interested in aesthetics for the sake of art, but in aesthetics for philosophy's sake."[6] Aestheticians are inspired by theory rather than art. They take as given for their reflection not artworks, but theoretical works constructed by their predecessors.

We find an ironic twist in the use of philosophic concepts by dance writers. Aestheticians derive many of their ideas not from direct experience with dance, but from books by dance writers (see Chapter 8). They selected from these written sources their primary data: the ideas which fit their aesthetic analytical model. Yet many dance writers derive their conceptual guidelines from aestheticians. Each group looks to the other for information; neither simply looks at dance itself as the starting point.

In the early part of the twentieth century the field of aesthetics underwent as radical a change as occurred in dance. Dance writers were unaware of this development. A revolution in philosophical discourse was triggered by Albert Einstein's theory of relativity. Applying the logical implications of Einstein's ideas, the influential philosopher Ludwig Wittgenstein challenged the previous belief in the definitive nature of language and showed that words had only relative, not absolute, meaning. Few people, he argued, would ever come to a lasting agreement on a closed, absolute definition of a word or concept; therefore the only viable way to discuss ideas is to offer operational definitions of words and to identify sets of salient features for concepts. Applying this method to analyses of the arts, most aestheticians concentrated on the study of sentient experience and the description of empirical data. This "scientific" or analytical method of analysis contrasted with the traditional "rational" method in which aestheticians responded to previous or prevalent theories.

Most serious students of dance were aware of the analysis of dance as an art by philosopher Susanne K. Langer, but they were unaware of the dance analyses written between 1920 and 1976 by at least thirteen other aestheticians. In this study, I assess the writing about dance of these fourteen aestheticians and the four dance theorists whose books served as influential sources for their consideration of dance. This evaluation reveals the patterns of their mutual influence and its consequences. This hitherto unnoticed influence enables us to reexamine the validity of pivotal theoretical dance writing of the early twentieth century.

The order of the chapters of *Dance-Based Dance Theory* reflects the mutual influence of each field. Langer and R.G. Collingwood contributed to the expression-communication theory of art in the rationalist tradition. This theory substantially influenced dance theorists Elizabeth Selden, John Martin, and Margaret H'Doubler. In turn, their books serve as source material for DeWitt Parker, Aram Torossian, Theodore M. Greene, Louis W. Flaccus, Thomas Munro, James K. Feibleman, Morris Weitz, Paul Weiss, Friedrich Kainz, Phillip Phenix, Etienne Gilson, and Alan Tormey. These eleven aestheticians write comparative studies of several arts including dance. A current leader in aesthetics, Nelson Goodman, depends in part for his understanding of dance upon the writings of Rudolf Laban, the dancer, choreographer, and theorist.

Many of the aestheticians' writings show they are unaware that their sources of dance theory are, in many ways, propaganda written to explain and defend the new "modern dance." These books have a strong anti-ballet bias and often attribute less value and prestige to the non-art dance forms. Hence, the picture of the field of dance in these books is not balanced. Another hidden problem lies in the way Selden, Martin, and H'Doubler simplify their aesthetic sources, just as the aestheticians select ideas from their dance sources to fit their analytical schemes.

The work of Laban does not fit this pattern. An examination of his theoretical work reveals the richness of his ideas inductively derived from in-depth dance experience. Since Laban's work provides a full analysis of dance from an internal dance viewpoint, his writings serve as a research and writing model for dance researchers and provide the criteria for my assessment of all the other writing discussed in this book.

This book, therefore, must also be about methodology for studying and writing about dance—all the dimensions of dance activities which constitute the academic field of dance. I aim to clarify the meaning, value, and concept of "dance theory." If we start with a working definition of "theory" as *an explanation of practice*, then we must examine, inductively, all parts of the field. We can also define the separate parts of dance in dance terms and show how they fit together in a truly comprehensive dance theory. Dance theory, my title asserts, must be derived from dance and not from sources other than dance.

Dance theorists regularly analyze, explain, and describe dance in writing. Their analyses are derived from the functions of dance: artistic, social-cultural, structural, historical, critical-descriptive, educational, therapeutic, and physical-physiological. Perceiving how these functions interrelate is the first step toward a comprehensive dance theory.

A useful definition of dance must be as complete as this comprehensive theory. Here is my operational definition of a dance:

> Dance activities are part of the cultural experience and expression of human beings. The physical activity, a dance, is recognized as a dance by the people doing and watching it. A dance is a sequence of bodily movements, usually composed and rehearsed. It is performed (danced) by people who assume the role of dancers, usually wearing special costumes.

These people often dance in selected spaces, such as on a theater stage, in a ballroom, or in a ceremonial setting, usually
accompanied by music or other sound. The dancing activity
usually occurs within a limited time frame, the dance event.
Dances are danced by people for several often overlapping
reasons: pleasure, aesthetic expression (as art), religious
worship, courtship, and play.

This definition incorporates all features of a dance event in its cultural and
historical setting; it is not a simple definition in answer to the question
"What is dance?" but includes features and dimensions in a complex picture of the event. The definition guides my evaluation of the writing of the
dance theorists and aestheticians.

We will view the ideas of these writers against a schematic framework of comprehensive dance theory, the Framework of Topics Intrinsic to
Dance Theory, which reflects the complex definition of a dance event.
Based on extensive personal as well as broad academic dance experience,
this Framework assembles the central topics which most of the writers in
this study discuss and organizes them into interrelated groupings. Chapter 2 introduces the Framework which then guides the analysis of the
writing of the fourteen aestheticians and four dance theorists whose studies of dance lay bare the pattern of mutual influence of dance and aesthetics.

The analysis which follows does not purport to argue the validity of
the works of the aestheticians on philosophic grounds. I am not a philosopher. I am a dance scholar who, by making the familiar strange, has observed a detrimental pattern in dance theory writing. Revealing the inadequacies of the writing by dance theorists and asetheticians in no way de-
nies the rich informative value of their work. My analysis reveals a serious flaw in academic dance practice, and is not meant to dismiss the field
of philosophy. Just as philosophy stands as an autonomous field, so must
dance.

NOTES

1 Naima Prevots, *American Pageantry: A Movement for Art and Democracy* (Ann Arbor, Mich.: UMI Research Press, 1990).

2 John Weaver, *An Essay Towards an History of Dancing* (London: J. Tomson, 1712), 160-161.

3 Louis de Cahusac, *La Danse Ancienne et Moderne* (La Haye: J. Neaulime, 1754).

4 Jean Georges Noverre, *Lettres sur La Danse et Les Ballets* (A. Lyon: Chez Aimé Delaroche, Imprimeur-Librairie du gouvernment & de la Ville aux Halles de la Grennette, 1760), tr. Cyril W. Beaumont under the title *Letters on Dancing and Ballet* (1930; rpt. Brooklyn, New York: Dance Horizons, 1966).

5 Carlo Blasis, *Traité Élémentaire, Théorique et Pratique de l'Art de la Danse* (Milan: Beauti et Tementi, 1820), tr. Mary Stewart Evans under the title *An Elementary Treatise upon the Theory and Practice of the Art of Dancing* (New York: Dover Publications, 1968).

6 Harry B. Lee, "The Cultural Lag in Aesthetics," *Journal of Aesthetics and Art Criticism*, 6 (1947), 121.

2

A FRAMEWORK FOR ANALYSIS AND EVALUATION

I have devised the Framework of Topics Intrinsic to Dance Theory to compare and contrast the writing of four dance theorists and fourteen aestheticians who wrote about dance between 1920 and 1976. Even though these eighteen thinkers wrote their books and chapters for a variety of academic reasons and from different philosophic schools, their discussions of dance are remarkably similar: they contain many of the same topics, they use similar terms to discuss these topics, they ponder similar questions, and they judge as central some of the same issues in their theoretical discussions of dance. Such similarity is not accidental: the aestheticians use the books of the dance theorists as source material, while the dance theorists model their writing on the aestheticians. I organize the topics considered by both groups of thinkers into general categories, add the topics they left out, and then arrange the groups of topics into a coherent interrelated framework.

The Framework of Topics Intrinsic to Dance Theory utilizes an inductive approach to analyze and evaluate dance theory. The Framework emerges out of the pooled ideas in the writings themselves; it does not impose theories, terms, or concepts from fields outside dance. The Framework interrelates the recognized branches of the study of dance: education, history, criticism, therapy, performance, design, ethnology, notation, choreography and identifies those theoretical issues shared and unique to each branch.[1] This comprehensive depiction of the field is not new; it is implied by the dance theorists examined in this study in that their analyses include almost all of the branches of dance. This Framework carries their ideas further by showing how the features of any kind of dance, be it modern dance, Tongon dance, or disco, relate to each other.

An insufficient number of physical examples of dance activities distinctly limits the writings about dance by the aestheticians and the dance theorists. The writers assume their readers have enough dance experience to comprehend a theoretical analysis of dance. The following pages contain a physical example to illustrate and define operationally the features of dance which both groups of writers assume their readers understand. The account employs the terms necessary for this analysis and it suggests how the features relate to each other.

Suppose a person felt the need to make up a skipping dance. He or she (she for simplicity) would experiment with many ways of skipping until she discovered a sequence of movements she liked. Her entire body, guided by her reason, emotions, and senses, all working in synchrony while she executes the dance movements is the *material* she uses in her skipping dance. Her *kinesthetic sense* guides her in exploring, selecting, and performing the movements of her dance. Perhaps, in addition to skipping, she selects jumping, running, and holding (momentarily stopping) movements. The tempos (*time* feature), the shapes, directions, and sizes of the movements (*space* feature), and the energies (*force* feature) that she chooses transform these ordinary everyday *movements* into *dance movements*.

Composing and performing a dance is the initial goal of the dance process. Once she stood up, skipped, and experimented with variations of the skip, jump, run, and hold sequence, she was in the *process* of composing a dance. The process of composing involves exploring (*improvisation*) and choosing movements, putting them into sequences, and then arranging them into a cohesive form. The process of arranging the movement sequences into an identifiable whole dance is similar to putting words into sentences, sentences into paragraphs, and paragraphs into a short story. *Choreography*, the process of composing, is both technical (using specific trained skills—*techniques*—and guidelines) and creative (original, discovered, unpredictable). When she practices skipping, running, and jumping to improve the way she performs these movements, she is working on her technique to train her physical skills. When she practices these movements to be able to repeat them exactly the way she intends, she is perfecting her performance technique. Internal guidelines (how the movements feel) and external guidelines (how the movements look) combine as the criteria guiding her performance.

If she decides to perform her dance for an audience, for ritual, social or theatrical purposes, she then teaches those movements to her fellow dancers and trains them to perform her skipping dance. She and her other dancers practice this sequence to project her dance to an audience, using performance techniques. If she sets the skipping dance to music, designs costumes for it, arranges stage lighting to provide an environment which highlights parts of the sequence, and constructs a set for the stage space, she is incorporating *other arts* to support and enhance her dance. The process of preparing for and staging the performance is called *production*. If her dance were for a ritual or social purpose, the production process is still necessary. Composing and rehearsing are usually done in private, whereas performing the dance is usually done for other people. The act of dancing, which requires constant physical exertion, also gives dancers pleasure as well as giving pleasure to the people watching. The physical activity of dancing the dance is central to the processes of making and performing it.

The movement sequence which the dancer completes, shows to a friend, teaches to other dancers, or performs for an audience is a dance. The *work*, the dance, is the entirety of all of the movements in motion from the beginning of the first skip to the dancer's final reach and hold. When she decided to show her dance to a friend, our choreographer changed the nature of her activity from movement exploration for her pleasure to a produced event to communicate her dance ideas to someone else. Communicating the *aesthetic intention* of the (dance)work is one of the main purposes of art.

"Aesthetic," a difficult term to define, describes a characteristic feature of an artwork: it is embedded in the work by virtue of the maker's intention to have the work seen as art and because the artist imposes a form on the raw material of the art—in this case body movements. "Aesthetic" also describes an attitude. Aesthetic experience is often stimulated by the beauty of some object, experience, or person. A British expert in aesthetic education, Malcolm Ross, defines aesthetic experience as a way of appreciating that includes awe, wonder, and even mystery.[2] As an example, consider an egg. How do we look at it? As food, if we are hungry; as a small container holding a chick embryo, if we are chicken farmers; and as a piece of sculpture, if we gaze at its shape, texture, size, and color all at once. We appreciate the arts for the aesthetic experiences they stimulate. An aesthetic component adheres even to social and ritual dances, in their unified shaped sequences, though this component is not their most significant feature.

When the dancer performed her dance, she did so with the intention to communicate its physical aesthetic meaning. Choreographers rarely articulate this aesthetic intention in words, though the title of a dance offers a hint. In social and ritual contexts the intention of the dance's originator is no less aesthetic but may focus more on playful or spiritual goals. The *aesthetic result*, experienced by an audience, is rarely articulated by its members beyond appreciation or displeasure.

Once the skipping dance is performed, the dancer can choose to forget it or to perform it many more times. She can use several tools to help remember her dance. To keep an accurate record of the movements of the dance, she can write down her dance in one of several systems of dance *notation*. Notating a dance requires careful analysis of all the elements of the movements: its time, its space, and its energy components. The score of a dance serves the same function as a musical score and makes it non-ephemeral. The score contains what a choreographer wants to be repeated. Once the skipping dance is scored, our dancer, or any other dancer who reads notation, can reconstruct her skipping dance after years of not dancing it. The dancers who dance in it are free to interpret the dance guided by the standards of their dance artistry and the choreographer's notated directions. Once a dance work is notated, then it can be understood as an entity and studied, apart from the choreographer, apart from the performance, apart from the choreographer's initial intention, and apart from the responses of the audience or critic to the choreographer's intention.

A dance can be *recorded* by film or videotape. These mechanical (as opposed to symbolic) media for recording a dance produce a duplicate of one performance of the dance work. Film and videotape function in the same way as do a phonograph record or an audiotape of a piece of music. These mechanical renditions of the dance record the dancers' specific interpretation. Such recordings are difficult to use for learning a dance and cumbersome to place side by side for comparative study; therefore, they have distinct physical and theoretical limitations.

We can identify the *participants* in this dance activity according to their roles. In the skipping dance, choreographer, dancer, and teacher, were, at one point, all the same person. The originator of the dance was the *choreographer*; when she danced it she also was the *dancer*; and when she taught her dance to the other dancers and directed their practice of the movements for the performance, she was the *teacher* of the dance work. All these roles can be separate. Sometimes choreographers never dance in their own dances, and once the dance is choreographed someone else may teach it to the performers.

Audiences and critics are *observers* of the the dance event. Dance *critics* articulate in words their informed though personal aesthetic response to the dance by describing and analyzing the elements of the dance work. Their ideas about the dance may clarify and illuminate the work for audience members and readers. This evaluator role may be played by many people, including the audience members, the dancers, and the producers. For social and ritual dance events, participants in the event also observe and evaluate the dance in some way.

Part I of the Framework of Topics of Intrinsic to Dance Theory organizes the features all dances have into three parts, which in reality are a unit: the experience of the dancer dancing the dance (fig. 1).

The Material	*The Process*	*The Work*
the dancer	*dancing*	*the dance*
body (total self)	technique	aesthetic intention
senses, especially	improvisation	aesthetic result
kinesthetic	composition	the dance notated
movement	performance	and recorded
dance movement	(produced)	
time, space	settings	
force	use of other arts	

Participants	*Observers*
dancer	audience
choreographer	critic
teacher	

FIGURE 1. Part I of the Framework.

In their discussions of the arts aestheticians have often divided the elements of art into three parts—the material, the process, and the work—though at times, they may emphasize one element more than the others in their theories. I found these categories useful in my examination of the topics considered by the dance theorists and the aestheticians in their theoretical analyses of dance.

The second part of the Framework (fig. 2) contains the applied and academic features of the these primary features of a dance event: their *functions* and their *study*. Whereas the "function" focusses on the uses and effects of a dance or dance activity on society, the "study" of dance provides explanations of the wide variations of dance functions found in the world.

The features of dance material can be studied. The individual movements of the skipping dance can be examined with the research tools and analytic methods used in the field of *kinesiology*. For instance, a kinesiologist might record and monitor the electrical impulses of each muscle group used in selected movements from the skipping dance. Kinesiologists apply formulae of biomechanics to analyze and explain human movement.

The processes of dance function as *therapy* and in *education*. The creative and technical parts of composition and performance can be taught with emphasis on the exploratory and experiential elements of the activity rather than on technique and performance training for professional goals. Improvisation can enhance the self-image of students in school settings and clients in rehabilitation settings because the exploratory process allows people to discover their abilities to control or free the flow of self-created movements and movement designs in space.

The many *systems of technique, methods of composition,* and *styles of performance* can also be studied. The several settings for dance such as a stage, a ballroom, a church, or a ritual space in a forest or field, each have a distinctive effect on the dance performance. All features of the process, including various production techniques, can be analyzed in their academic, recreational, and professional contexts.

Any dance work comes about because some human being felt the need to express something in movement terms. In most human societies, dances, as completed works, function in several ways. Ballroom, folk, and square dancing provide *recreation* for those who participate. Concert dance and dance as parts of musical comedy, opera, films, videotapes, and night club acts provide *entertainment* for many people. Parades, weddings, funerals, and graduations all share the processional march, a vestige of ancient *religious* dance rituals. A thorough study of any time in the history of a society would show dances functioning in these ways along with their function as an art.

The dance scholar, using research methods adapted from several academic disciplines, can study many dimensions of the dance work itself. Perhaps the choreographer repeated the skipping dance as a ritual every day before work. The dance scholar could analyze the purpose of the dance in religious, sociological, or psychological terms. The scholar could investigate pre-work dances in other cultures, in the South Seas for instance. Using anthropological research methods, the scholar could compare the pre-work skipping ritual to other pre-work rituals or study its

	Functions of the Process in education in therapy	*Functions of the Work* in recreation in religion or ritual in entertainment
Material Studied kinesiology	*Process Studied* systems of technique methods of composition styles of performance	*Work Studied* past cultural contexts present cultural contexts

Viewpoints

dancer	scholar
choreographer	critic
teacher	audience
therapist	

FIGURE 2. Part II of the Framework.

history. Research methods from history, anthropology, sociology, and psychology can be modified to fit the study of dances in their cultural contexts.

Features and functions of dances are studied by dancers, choreographers, critics, scholars, teachers, therapists, theorists, and audiences from within their own and from other perspectives. I call these perspectives "viewpoints." The different viewpoints may overlap and combine. The people who view and understand dance as art respond to it according to a combination of their personal, professional, aesthetic, and cultural criteria. People participating in and watching ritual-religious and social-recreational dances also respond to those forms of dance with a combination of such criteria.

With the essential features of any dance event identified, the Framework is useful in analyzing and evaluating the theoretical writing discussed in this or any dance-related book. This analysis and evaluation requires the following steps. First, we look for the inclusion of all of the features in each category of the Framework. This step reveals how thorough the discussion is in a given text. Secondly, since the features are interconnected and interdependent, the Framework allows us to test how these interdependencies are described and analyzed. The Framework begins from inside the dancer-choreographer's experience but it includes other points of view, such as those of the audience, critic, and scholar. The Framework, therefore, generates evaluative criteria for assessing any writing about dance. Admittedly, material not included in the Framework and not relevant to the discussion of dance is omitted.

FRAMEWORK OF TOPICS INTRINSIC TO DANCE THEORY

The Material	*The Process*	*The Work*
(the tools: the dancer)	*(the method: dancing)*	*(the product: a dance)*
body	technique	aesthetic intention
senses, especially	improvisation	aesthetic result
kinesthetic	composition	the dance notated
movement	performance	and recorded
dance movement	(produced)	
time, space	settings	
force	use of other arts	

Participants	*Observers*
dancer	audience
choreographer	critic
teacher	

	Functions of	*Functions of*
	the Process	*the Work*
	in education	in recreation
	in therapy	in religion or ritual
		in entertainment

Material Studied	*Process Studied*	*Work Studied*
kinesiology	systems of technique	past cultural
	methods of	contexts
	composition	present cultural
	styles of performance	contexts

Viewpoints

dancer	scholar
choreographer	critic
teacher	audience
therapist	

FIGURE 3. The Complete Framework

NOTES

[1] Alma Hawkins, "A Look at the Future," in *Dance: A Projection for the Future*, ed. Marian Van Tuyl (San Francisco: Impulse Publications, 1968). These categories are in a chart on page 99.

[2] Malcolm Ross, *The Aesthetic Impulse* (Oxford: Pergamon Press, 1981), 145.

3

DANCE IN THE AESTHETIC THEORY OF
R. G. COLLINGWOOD

If the Framework of Topics Intrinsic to Dance Theory is a useful analytic tool, then it will facilitate the examination of ideas about dance by scholars in any field. We start with the ideas about dance by R. G. Collingwood (1889–1943) because his aesthetic theory was among the first twentieth-century versions of the expression-communication explanation of art. Little known to dance scholars, Collingwood's work preceded Langer's by four years. He held a prestigious chair of philosophy at Oxford University during the first half of the twentieth century and was well known for his work in the philosophy of history. His *Principles of Art* (1938) expands on Benedetto Croce's turn-of-the-century theory of art as an expression of the imagination.[1] Developing Croce's ideas, Collingwood emphasizes the artist's expression of emotion as formulated by the mind, then communicated by way of the art product to make an aesthetic effect on the audience. He sorts art proper from bad art, art falsely so called, and art from craft. For him the arts, like language, express universal ideas and feelings. Verbal language, Collingwood argues, is just one of many ways of communicating, and all forms of communication stem from bodily feeling.

Collingwood's theory encompasses abstract expression in all the arts. Such developments as symbolic logic, stream of consciousness novels, free verse, atonal music, abstract painting, and modern dance, he asserts, are new ways of expressing emotions. Symbolic logic reveals inner patterns of reasoning, stream of consciousness writing gleans from concrete experience a variety of described inner properties, free verse and modern dance formulate unique structures to convey emotional content, abstract painting changes and distorts reality and then renders it in new forms, or even creates from fantasy in imaginary free-form designs. Collingwood's analysis of abstraction encompasses each of these forms. When he wrote, artists and scientists were seeking new vehicles to express their changing understanding of reality, while critics resisted these new concepts. One of Collingwood's primary reasons for writing *Principles of Art* was to explain how contemporary innovations would be immediately understood as art by the public.

Collingwood's mode of aesthetic inquiry is to build a closed and closely reasoned theory in which he asks such questions as: What is art? What is not art? What does it mean? How does it communicate? He extracts obsolete, analogical, and courtesy meanings from the primary use of the word "art." Collingwood intends his theory to be complete and allows for no exceptions. In the philosophic tradition, if a critic identifies one exception, correction, or inaccuracy in any part, the theory as a whole is discredited. Dance is central to Collingwood's theory of art; the Framework of Topics Intrinsic to Dance Theory facilitates an examination of the comprehensiveness and accuracy of his ideas about dance.

The Material

Collingwood's understanding of the *material* of dance is thorough because he incorporates the body, all the senses including the kinesthetic, and body movement. For Collingwood the body and its movements are a means to an end, the source and vehicle of the emotions which the mind formulates into art experiences. Like all physical components of the arts, the body for Collingwood is merely a vehicle for the imagined art experience.

Our source of consciousness, according to Collingwood, is bodily activity. Any movement expressed in any form is a manifestation of internal feelings. Experience first arises in our bodies. It is then converted by our consciousness from physical impression and sensation to an idea in our imagination: "The language of total bodily gesture is thus the motor side of our total imaginative experience" (247). The most commonly perceived language, Collingwood observes, is vocal speech. Speech is a system of particular gestures which produce characteristic sounds perceived through the ear and the eye. Thus Collingwood identifies the relationships among body, mind, and language.

Different kinds of language, he asserts, are all related to bodily gesture. The painter's gestures while painting contribute to the artwork, and the musician's muscles, breath, and eye movements all participate in music making. Likewise, the eyes of the viewer of a painting rove over its tactile pathways, just as the listener to music vicariously dances to its sounds. In this way, all languages are specialized forms of bodily gesture. Therefore, Collingwood argues, all languages are an off-shoot of the original language of total bodily gesture. Gesture is central to all forms of expression, even in rigidity and silence. In fact, he asserts, all movement is a type of dance movement. To Collingwood, dance, "the mother of all languages" (244), is the basic and primary form of communication.

The kinesthetic sense, according to him, is basic to communication and thus is central to all art experience. Because of our body's sensitivity to expressive movement, many intense emotions are infectious. When we see someone who is hurt or hear that person groaning, the pain of the other produces an echo we can feel in our own bodies: our animal sympathy allows pain to be contagious. This muscular-emotional sensitivity is the source of dance material, the means of communicating dance to others, and the means by which audience members receive the communication.

Collingwood's theory unites the mind and body; this common philosophical dichotomy is absent from his writing. Internal experience is the source of movement for dance, and the kinesthetic sense is a primary means for experiencing, expressing, and responding to internal and external communication. Primarily because his viewpoint is as an outsider to dance, Collingwood only touches on how and why physical sensation can stimulate action when it registers in our consciousness.

Participants

Collingwood uses the word "artist" (we could substitute the word "dancer") to mean both creator and performer. The artist is a specialist who expresses art experiences for the community. He makes only one reference to teaching, when he touches upon the hard work involved in art making. Because expression-communication is central in Collingwood's theory of art, he minimizes the creative process of making the artwork and focuses on the performing (recreative) process of communicating.

Process

Though rudimentary, Collingwood's thinking about the *process* includes technique, composition, and performance. He considers the internal motivation for art and then carries the process all the way to its completed production before an audience. Collingwood's discussion of how technique contributes to art applies directly to dance. Great artists, he asserts, can produce fine art with defective technique but perfect technique cannot substitute for great art. Good technical skill, on the whole, will contribute to good works of art but should not call attention to itself. For Collingwood, technique is part of craft and is less important than the art expression itself, though he sees it as necessary for good art: technique is a means to an end.

Collingwood identifies three steps in the process of making a work of art. First, the artist becomes conscious of an internally sensed experience he or she wants to communicate. Collingwood organizes these steps in the context of a musician's creative process: when the tune is only in the musician's head it is already complete and perfect as an imaginary tune.

In the second step, a combination of production and performance, the musician arranges for the tune to be played for an audience. The real tune now exists as a collection of noises. This art object is now in some sense physical by being outside the musician's head. During the third step, the audience discerns and receives the noises: "The noises made by the performers and heard by the audience are not music at all; they are only means by which the audience, if they listen intelligently (not otherwise), can reconstruct for themselves the imaginary tune that existed in the composer's head" (193). Substitute "movements" for "noises," "see" for "listen," and "dance" for "music" and this description can apply to dance. This sequence of events—inspiration, composition-production, and communication—summarizes Collingwood's understanding of art experience, "an imagined experience of total activity" (151).

Only once does Collingwood analyze how artists learn to express meaning, to "convert . . . the psychical experience into an imaginative one" (232). In a discussion separate from the three-step expression-communication sequence above, he identifies the missing creative process when he claims artists teach themselves how to meet their own internally set standards: "What the student learns in an art school is not so much to paint as to watch himself painting: to raise the psycho-physical activity of painting to the level of art by becoming conscious of it" (281).

Can art in general (and dance in particular) exist without an audience? All arts, Collingwood argues, are performing arts, thus they are incomplete without an audience. Artists, he claims, externalize art ideas to share with other people who do not choose to engage in art activity. Audience members collaborate with the artist; they participate actively by doing it over again in their minds. This audience-artist interdependence is especially true for dance because a dance, a performing art, is complete only after all the processes of choreographing, teaching, rehearsing, staging, and performing are accomplished.

The Framework of Topics Intrinsic to Dance Theory enables us to analyze the strengths and weaknesses of Collingwood's analysis of the artistic creative process. He minimizes composition, the difficult work of formalizing the art conception into the finished art work. He exaggerates the communication aspect of the artwork and thereby diminishes the importance of the art itself in providing the mechanism for this communication.

Observers

The manner by which dance or any art is received by the audience is that basic way people receive any communication from within themselves or from the outside. Every variation of emotion to which the psyche responds, Collingwood insists, is first experienced in the muscles and in the internal organs. For the audience members to understand dance (or another art) aesthetically, they must be receptive through their kinesthetic sense.

Collingwood addresses critics and audiences when he proposes a way to discriminate between bad art and art falsely so called. In a bad work of art, an artist has tried to express an emotion but failed; "In art falsely so called there is no failure to express, because there is only an attempt (whether successful or not) to do something else" (282). He urges critics and audience members to become sensitive to the difference between bad and false art.

The Work

Collingwood's analysis of the *work* follows logically from his understanding of the *process* and magnifies its flaws. The artwork results from the organized and externalized imagined experience of the artist, communicated to an audience. "A work of art proper," he asserts, "is total activity which the person enjoying it apprehends, or is conscious of, by the use of his imagination" (151). The work, therefore, is a means to an end; the end is communication of the artist's expression.

According to Collingwood, the process of communication determines art proper because, unlike craft which displays its technique, art proper is a deliberate form of expression. Artists express emotions comprehensible to the people participating in the art experience who must believe the emotional expression of the artist to be their own. Artists are not special because they convincingly express their emotions; they are uniquely able to initiate the expression of commonly felt emotions. For Collingwood, artists directly share expressive content with others by way of art proper. Indeed, the *work* is instrumental to the expression-communication, indistinguishable from the *process* and incomplete without *observers*.

The Functions of the Work and the Work Studied

Collingwood distinguishes among dance performance in art, entertainment, and magic. He analyzes how each type of performance functions: entertainment provides catharsis, magic channels energy to practical life, and art communicates the artist's expression to an audience. He goes on to demonstrate how each setting coordinates with its function, though he does not discuss each dance type in detail because his analysis centers on differentiating art from non-art in general terms.

Dance as entertainment includes elements of magic with distinguishable differences. Entertainment fits Collingwood's characterization of craft since it utilizes traditional steps, music, and costumes; it highlights their formal aspects, their outward appearances, their sensational appeal, and their decorative value. The make-believe in magic functions to guide practical life, not to divert attention from it as in entertainment. The main difference between magic, entertainment, and art lies in theatrical "illusion"; make-believe is always found in magic and entertainment, but never, Collingwood asserts, in art proper. Collingwood offers a guideline to distinguish between art and entertainment: when the audience attends to a performer's skill or reacts in a predictable way to a given stimulus, then the performance is entertainment.

Collingwood illustrates historical acumen when he points out how recreational forms of dance have vestiges of ritual from the past. He identifies ballroom dancing as a contemporary courtship-ritual where socially compatible young men and women come together to choose future mates. His knowledge about the functions of dance in ritual, courtship, and entertainment demonstrates a sensitivity to dance detail unusual in a general aesthetic theory.

Collingwood's theory of art illustrates both the power of philosophic discourse, as in his argument that dance is the mother of all languages, and the weakness of philosophic reasoning, for dance or any art, according to Collingwood, is only a means to an end and not important for its own sake. Few members of the dance community refer to Collingwood's philosophic ideas about dance. Had they become acquainted with his work, they would have been pleased to find Collingwood building his entire theory around the many communicative variations of dance, and they would have been reassured about the status of dance as art. Dance, for Collingwood, is not just *an* art, but the common denominator of all arts.

His theoretical mode, however, limits the comprehensiveness of his theory. He proposes one simple definition of art and limits the meanings of terms on which he builds his theory. And, because they are not pertinent to his argument, he leaves out essential features of dance, such as improvisation, production, notation, and dance teaching.

NOTE

[1] R. G. Collingwood, *The Principles of Art* (1938; rpt. London: Oxford University Press, 1974). Page references to this work in this chapter will be inserted parenthetically in the text.

4

DANCE IN THE AESTHETIC THEORY OF
SUSANNE K. LANGER

Susanne K. Langer, a contemporary of Collingwood, was a highly regarded American philosopher who taught at Columbia University and Connecticut College for Women. In her book *Feeling and Form* (1953), she devotes two chapters, "Virtual Powers" and "The Magic Circle," to dance.[1] The ideas in these chapters, summarized in her chapter on dance in *Problems of Art* (1957), have had major impact on dance scholarship. Shortly after *Feeling and Form* came out, dance scholars, teachers, and students eagerly adopted Langer's ideas about dance by quoting her in their writings, teaching "Dance Philosophy" courses based on her ideas, and applying her ideas in their theoretical books.[2] For example, Maxine Sheets-Johnstone in *The Phenomenology of Dance* and Eleanor Metheny in *Movement and Meaning* accepted Langer's theory and built their theories on it.[3] Langer's ideas were popular because dance people needed to prove the value of writing about such an apparently ethereal subject, while adding academic validity to their theses about dance as an art. The value of Langer's recognition of dance far outweighed the limitations of her theory. A few dance scholars (Irmgard Bartenieff, Selma Jeanne Cohen, Judith L. Hanna, and Judith B. Alter) have criticized major features of Langer's theory, but her ideas remain popular in the dance community.[4]

Though only a few dance scholars who have argued against some of Langer's ideas, at least twelve philosophers have criticized pivotal ideas in her theory of art.[5] Leading philosophers Ernest Nagel and Morris Weitz conclusively demonstrated the inaccurate and inadequate premises on which she built her arguments, yet dance scholars have remained unaware of these and other criticisms of her work. Although the insights of the philosopher critics of Langer aid this analysis of her ideas about dance, the Framework of Topics Intrinsic to Dance Theory provides a dance-based method to evaluate her theory.

Langer is among the aestheticians who espoused the expression-communication theory of art popular earlier in this century. In contrast to Collingwood, in whose interpretation art expresses emotions, Langer claims art expresses ideas about human feeling. Her arguments place her on the rational side of the pendulum swing between the rational and emotional function of art, an ongoing debate in the field of aesthetics. In an earlier book, *Philosophy in a New Key* (1942), Langer divides ways of communicating into two categories: discursive symbolism of which language is an example, where words are analogous to the ideas for which they stand, and presentational symbolism of which music, dance, architecture, and the other arts are examples.[6] Dance as art is "the creation of forms expressive of human feeling" (60).

Ernest Nagel identifies the flaws in her notion of language: Words, as discursive symbols, and their meanings may symbolically exemplify the concepts they represent, Nagel argues, but they are not analogous to those concepts. He identifies a contradiction in her notion of art as presentational symbols. Although she claims presentational symbols differ from discursive symbols, Nagel argues that for arts to be "symbols" of sense experience, the symbol must stand for something. Arts, she claims, reflect the "morphology of feeling" and this means they convey *general* forms of feeling. But earlier she claimed that discursive—not presentational—symbols do that. Nagel's arguments show the inaccuracy of Langer's definitions of discursive and presentational symbols.[7]

In her next book, *Feeling and Form* (1953), Langer builds on this mistaken definition of two discrete categories of symbols. She focusses on the primary illusion created by the symbolism in a work of art. Like Collingwood, Langer applies closed definitions to the terms on which she bases her arguments. Art, for Langer, stands out from the everyday world and has unique qualities, or "import," which cause it to contrast with daily reality. Artworks are logically expressive of human feelings by their presentation of an image or symbol.

Haig Khatchadourian recognizes the inaccuracy of Langer's idea about how artworks "express feelings." Works of art themselves do not express merely the artist's feelings or emotions. The creative act of an artist involves many feelings and much work, reasoning, and crafting. Artworks stimulate or convey emotions and feelings in audiences, but as inanimate objects they are incapable of "expressing" anything.[8] Louis Arnaud Reid argues a similar point. An artist does not express "what he knows 'about' human feeling. It sounds as if he were a kind of information bureau, specializing in what is called 'life of feeling.'"[9] Like Collingwood, Langer oversimplifies the reality of the artist's creative processes.

Langer believes the main task of the artist is "to produce and sustain the essential illusion, set it off clearly from the surrounding world of actuality and articulate its form to the point where it coincides unmistakably with forms of feeling and living" (68). Richard Norton challenges Langer's notion of art as an "illusion" or a "virtual reality." Anything virtual or illusory, he contends, is connected to reality.[10] Langer's separation of the dynamic illusion from the bodies producing the dance illusion creates the same mistake as separating "form" from "content."

Langer identifies the primary illusion of dance to be a *virtual realm of power*. She intends to correct the mistaken definitions and the misuses of dance "linked with amusement, dressing-up, frivolity . . . and religion, terror, mysticism, and madness." She is emphatic that "dance, no matter how diverse its phases and how multifarious, perhaps even undignified its uses, is unmistakably and essentially art, and performs the functions of art in worship as in play" (184). For her dance readers, this sentence declaring dance to be "unmistakably" an art is the significant one in a field struggling for recognition.

Like Norton, Morris Weitz, in his review of *Feeling and Form*, attacks Langer's attempt to reduce each art to a single, controlling element, its primary illusion. Weitz sees her reductionistic theory as a throwback to earlier versions of formalism. He questions the goal of her theory: "Mrs. Langer likes her categories neat, and everything in all the arts falls, with an invigorating dexterity, into its assigned place. But throughout one keeps wondering whether she is talking about the arts or her own interlocking set of categories."[11] Weitz demonstrates how Langer distorts or leaves out essential features of each of the arts she analyzes because her overriding focus is on finding the primary illusion of each one. In the context of her theory of art Langer's distortion of dance follows her analytical model, but when dance writers took it out of context for use in dance theory, the oversights and distortions of her theory were magnified.

The Material

Langer includes in her discussion of dance the components of the basic material: body, the senses, especially the kinesthetic sense, everyday movement, and dance movement. For Langer the dancer's moving body is the stimulus which creates the illusion of virtual power. Dancers use their highly developed kinesthetic sense in dancing. They also utilize their rhythmic ability while kinesthetically conceptualizing dance.

The primary material of dance, for Langer, is gesture, "the basic abstraction whereby the dance illusion is made and organized" (174). Dancers, she realizes, choose their dance movements from everyday gestures. Because Langer claims the expression of dance movement is logical and not physical or emotional, she corrects Laban's explanation of dance materials as a combination of the physical, the emotional, and the conceptual:

> But as one remembers that the statements Laban makes about emotions refer to *body feelings*, physical feelings that spring from the *idea* of an emotion and initiate symbolic gestures which articulate this idea, and that his "emotional forces" are semblances of physical or magical forces, one can turn his specious physical account of the world and its energies into a description of the illusory realm of "powers," and then his analyses all make sense. (186)

Laban's multi-dimensional explanation does not fit Langer's theory; thus she extracts from his ideas the conceptual feature to fit her rational definition of dance. Irmgard Bartenieff sharply criticizes Langer's reinterpretation of Laban's ideas as simply the mistaken mind-body dualism.[12] Langer's use of Laban's idea typifies her selective interpretation of her other dance sources. Since dance is the symbolic condition (logically expressive) not the symptom of existing conditions (self-expressive), gesture "appears as visible motion but not a motion of things, sliding, waving or rolling around—it is seen and understood as vital movement" (175). Thus, she understands the physical aspect of dance only as its source and not as an integral part of the actual dance. Although Langer discusses the body, the senses, everyday movement, and dance movement in her analysis of dance, she limits the accuracy of her analysis because she writes from the audience point of view.

The Process

Langer's audience point of view also limits her examination of the dance *process*. She considers only some features of dance technique, composition, and performance. Her single comment about technique concerns its contribution to artistic communication: The better the technique, Langer acknowledges, the better the dancer is able to express the power of a dance.

When considering composition and performance, Langer rejects the notion of dance as "a free discharge of either surplus energy or of emotional excitement"; instead, she claims that "imagined feeling . . . governs dance" (177). She acknowledges that this notion of virtual emotion differing from real feelings can prove confusing for artists because they have the hardest time separating their own imagined world from the real one. Even with philosophical training, "the very notion of feeling and emotion not really felt, but only imagined is strange to most people" (181). If one imagines feeling, she reasons, then it is not felt but experienced in the mind, hence it is rational rather than emotional. This dichotomy of reason and emotion traps aestheticians into arguments which cannot be resolved: while creating, artists employ a combination of their rational and emotional faculties.

Langer's fellow philosopher Eugene Kaelin exposes the fallacy of the notion of feelings not being felt by audience or dancer but only "understood." He argues, "To suggest that a dancer first understands a feeling, and then translates it into kinesthetic imagery, is to suggest that a dancer dances before dancing; since the counters of the dance medium are movements, the dancer must already have made the movements in order to have gained his or her 'idea.'"[13] Although at times ideas motivate dancers to choreograph, they select movements for their dances by improvising until they find the best movements to express their ideas. Langer's theory leaves out the physical experience from the choreographer's point of view.

When describing the unique characteristics of a performed dance, Langer distinguishes dance from music, pictures in motion, and pantomime. When she examines the compositional elements of dance (space, time, and fantasy), she acknowledges these to be features of other arts as well as dance. Langer is also aware how other arts, especially music, combine with dances in their production.

She sums up her understanding of a performed dance in terms of other arts:

> The primary illusion of dance is a peculiarly rich experience ...
> Both space and time are implicitly created with it. Story runs
> through it like a thread, without linking it at all to literature;
> impersonation and miming are often systematically involved
> in its basic abstraction, virtual gesture, but dance pantomime
> is not drama; the mummery of masks and costumes to which
> its thematic gestures belong is depersonalizing rather than
> humanly interesting . . . . Its space is plastic, its time is musi-
> cal, its themes are fantasy, its actions symbolic. (204)

Here Langer incorporates the way dance utilizes elements of the other arts and astutely grasps the multilayered nature of dance as a theater art. Her audience point of view, in this case, enables her to conceptualize dance in its complex richness.

Selma Jeanne Cohen is critical of Langer's separation of the body from the image it creates during a performance, asserting, "we *do* see what is before us even though the effect of the dance, when it succeeds, projects an energy, an ambience, a significance that is more than the sum of the events we observe occurring in time and space."[14] Langer's notion of dance movement as an illusion created by moving bodies, Cohen and Bartenieff agree, is only a partial truth. In reality, dance is physical, and audiences cannot see the patterns of moving bodies unless the bodies are actually moving in space in the performance setting.

Langer's examination of the process of dance training, composing, and producing is incomplete, because she leaves out the technical and cre- ative process a choreographer must go through to compose a dance. She focusses on the rational dimension by envisioning the emotional expres- sion of the artist as symbolic depersonalized feeling. Her exaggeration of the rational over the other dimensions of dance may be appropriate in her philosophic enterprise, but applied to dance theory, her vision of dance is imbalanced.

Observers

Dance, Langer argues, needs an audience to become art. She believes audience members understand art symbols by means of a *Gestalt* response and utilize their kinesthetic, visual, and aural senses in that experience of dance. Her analysis of dance emphasizes the audience because in her interpretation of the expression-communication theory, the art process is only complete when audience members comprehend the symbolic meaning of the performance.

The Work

True dance for Langer is conceptual. She quotes dance writers to support this contention: Curt Sachs thinks dance is a symbolic world, and Merle Armitage claims it is form (178).[15] In discussing "so-called 'Modern Dance,'" Langer thinks self-expression is only a motif like any other motif (181). The actual dance, for Langer, is neither gestural rendering of music or animated design: it is virtual gesture conveying symbolic emotions. What is seen, she argues, is virtual like a rainbow—it exists in effect, but not in fact. The visual design made by the moving bodies is the dance. In this proposition she is separating the part, the visual design, from the whole, the dancer making the design by dancing, implying that the part is the whole. Langer views dance as a member of the audience: from this perspective she extracts only the impact of seeing a dance.

For Langer, dance as an illusion becomes a free symbolic form conveying ideas of emotion in combination with gestures expressing other physical and mental tensions. Dance gestures, she contends, are symbols of will even though they appear spontaneous and physical. The images of any performance seen at the moment of performing are "virtual" to the audience, but Langer fails to acknowledge that the illusion the audience members see cannot exist without the physically created design and energy of the performers who project the dance. Langer's theory, like Collingwood's, regards the dance as a mere instrument for the communication of the artist's concepts.

The Work Studied

Langer shows awareness of past styles of dance composition in her discussion of what true dance is. Dance, she claims, is not the gestural rendering of musical forms, even if some dancers and musicians say it is. Dance is not simply "one of the plastic arts, a spectacle of shifting pictures or animated design, statues in motion," (172) even if neo-classic dancers of the 1910s and 1920s felt it should be that. Nor is dance pantomime, though pantomime can provide dance material.

Langer considers all the categories of dance to be creative and not athletic—an unnecessary distinction. The title of art, she argues, applies broadly to all dancing of any tradition or style, sacred or secular, including cult, folk, ballroom, ballet, and modern expressive dance. While her concept of dance incorporates its many functions and forms, it continues to envision dance solely from the audience rather than from the dancer's point of view as well.

To buttress her theory of art, Langer interprets human history as a progressive social development from primitive to modern, and from mythic to philosophic and scientific thinking. She accepts three progressive historical stages of dance: dance in religious ritual, folk communal dance, and spectacular theater dance. The third stage she pronounces the most advanced because dance addressed to an audience becomes deliberately a spectacle. As a spectacle the true creative aim—to make the world of powers visible—is achieved. For Langer, all forms of dance are creative to some extent because they transform gesture into visible powers; thus even social dancing is an art, if the dancers project their gestures convincingly to the spectators as virtual powers.

Langer depends on Curt Sachs for her interpretation of dance history. As Suzanne Youngerman demonstrates, because Sachs espouses the outdated developmental theory of history, his work was too narrowly selective.[16] Langer does not recognize the factual limitations of Sachs' book because his views help her achieve her goal of identifying the essential characteristic of dance (powers or great illusions) in all types of dance throughout the history of dance.

Langer's Legacy: the Ephemerality of Dance

Langer's theory of dance includes most of the topics of the Framework. She values the rich aesthetic experience of watching a dance performance no matter what its function or setting, yet she fails to examine all the features of dance because of her audience point of view. Her closed definitions of dance concepts place unfortunate constraints on complex ideas she hoped to clarify: a dance as not physical, but only the "virtual" visual design; choreographic motivation as only imagined not actually felt; and all forms of dance as art. The primary message dance writers take from Langer is the ephemerality of dance. Since all performing arts are ephemeral in their performance, that feature is only one part of the complex physical, aesthetic, conceptual, and emotional existence of performed dance. Her mode of thinking deceptively limits her conceptualization to an outside viewpoint from which to analyze each of the dance-art phenomena she discusses.

Aestheticians who espouse the expression-communication theory of art understand the work of art as an instrument through which the artist's aesthetic intention is expressed—Collingwood's focus—or through which the ephemeral hoped for communication process is achieved—Langer's emphasis. Collingwood and Langer both believe audiences grasp art directly, through a *Gestalt* response (Langer) or through contagion (Collingwood). Though Langer believes symbols, bearing their ideas, present their illusion by standing out from reality, she does not explain how they communicate their ideas. Collingwood does not explain how contagion, through the kinesthetic sense, facilitates the audience's understanding of what the artist is expressing by means of the art product. Collingwood overemphasizes the artist's expressive process, while Langer gives too much weight to the rational, symbolic, and ephemeral aesthetic result of the dance.

Langer, like Collingwood, valued dance as an art and wrote eloquently about it at a time when leaders of the dance community were searching for public and academic recognition of their art. For those readers, the theoretical limitations and factual inaccuracies of her theory were unimportant compared to the academic status her writing provided them; thus, they did not examine her ideas carefully. Their own dance theorists—John Martin, Elizabeth Selden, Margaret H'Doubler, and Rudolf Laban—though valued, cited, and recommended in writings on dance, were valued less (like family), since they were not recognized as professional philosophers.

NOTES

1 Susanne K. Langer, *Feeling and Form* (New York: Scribner's Sons, 1953). Page references to this book in this chapter will be indicated parenthetically in the text.

2 Ernestine Stodelle, "A Dancer's Philosopher: Susanne K. Langer," *Dance Observer*, 30 (1963), 69-70.

3 Maxine Sheets-Johnstone, *The Phenomenology of Dance* (Madison, Wis.: University of Wisconsin Press, 1966), and Eleanor Metheny, *Movement and Meaning* (New York: McGraw-Hill, 1968).

4 Irmgard Bartenieff, "The Roots of Laban Theory: Aesthetics and Beyond," in *Four Adaptations of Effort Shape Theory in Research and Teaching* ed. I.M. Bartenieff, M. Davis, and F. Pauley (New York: Dance Notation Bureau, 1970) 1-28; Selma Jeanne Cohen, *Next Week, Swan Lake* (Middletown, Conn.: Wesleyan University Press, 1982); Judith L. Hanna, *To Dance Is Human* (Austin: University of Texas Press, 1979); and Judith B. Alter, "A Critical Analysis of Susanne K. Langer's Dance Theory," in *A Spectrum of World Dance*, Dance Research Annual 16, ed. L. A. Wallen and J. Acocella (New York: Congress on Research in Dance, 1987), 110-119.

5 David Best, *Expression in Movement and the Arts* (London: Lepus Books, 1974); Richard Courtney, "On Langer's Dramatic Illusion," *Journal of Aesthetics and Art Criticism*, 29 (1970), 11-20; Eugene Kaelin, *Art and Existence* (Lewisburg, Pa.: Bucknell University Press, 1970); Haig Khatchadourian, "The Expression Theory of Art: A Critical Evaluation," *Journal of Aesthetics and Art Criticism*, 23 (1965), 335-352; Ernest Nagel, review of *Philosophy in a New Key*, *Journal of Philosophy*, 40 (1943), 323-329; Richard Norton, "What Is Virtuality?," *Journal of Aesthetics and Art Criticism*, 30 (1972), 499-505; Louis Arnaud Reid, "Feeling and Expression in the Arts: Expression, Sense and Feelings," *Journal of Aesthetics and Art Criticism*, 25 (1966), 123-135; Louis Arnaud Reid, "Susanne Langer and Beyond," *British Journal of Aesthetics*, 5 (1965), 357-367; Max Reiser, "The Semantic Theory of Art in America," *Journal of Aesthetics and Art Criticism*, 15 (1956), 12-26; Richard Rudner, "On Semiotic Aesthetics," *Journal of Aesthetics and Art Criticism*, 10 (1951), 67-77; Arthur Szathmary, "Symbolic and

Aesthetic Expression in Painting," *Journal of Aesthetics and Art Criticism* 13 (1954), 86-96; Morris Weitz, "Symbolism and Art," *Review of Metaphysics*, 7 (1954), 466-481; Robert L. Zimmerman, "Can Anything Be an Aesthetic Object?," *Journal of Aesthetics and Art Criticism* 25 (1966), 177-186.

[6] Susanne K. Langer, *Philosophy in a New Key* (Cambridge, Mass.: Harvard University Press, 1942), 79-102.

[7] Nagel, review of *Philosophy in a New Key*, 323-329.

[8] Khatchadourian, 335-352.

[9] Reid, "Feeling and Expression in the Arts," 301.

[10] Norton, 505.

[11] Weitz, 473.

[12] Bartenieff, 9.

[13] Kaelin, 149.

[14] Cohen, 110.

[15] Curt Sachs, *World History of the Dance* (New York: W. W. Norton, 1937).

[16] Suzanne Youngerman, "Curt Sachs and His Heritage: A Critical Review of *World History of the Dance* with a Survey of Recent Studies that Perpetuate His Ideas" *CORD News*, 1-2 (1974), 6-19.

5

THE DANCE THEORY OF
ELIZABETH SELDEN

The influence of the expression-communication theory of art is found in the writing of dance theorists Elizabeth Selden, John Martin, and Margaret H'Doubler. As advocates for the new expressive (as opposed to spectacular) dance form, they used the vocabulary of this theory to help articulate their message: modern dance communicates universal experience through internally motivated original movement vocabulary and deep emotional content.

Dancer, choreographer, dance critic, theorist, and teacher Elizabeth Selden (1888–19??) wrote her books of dance theory because, she writes, "nobody would write for me when I needed it, in my training years."[1] Her training included twenty years of study or work with Isadora Duncan, Mary Wigman, Rudolf Laban, Maja Lex, Michio Ito, Harold Kreutzberg, Doris Humphrey, Martha Graham, and Margaret Gage in major cities on several continents. After her studies, she directed the dance activities at Bennett School in New York for five years. She published two books, *Elements of the Free Dance* (1930) and a collection of essays written between 1926 and 1935 called *The Dancer's Quest* (1935). She correctly claims this collection to be among the first inclusive technical discussions of modern dance theory. In both her books, Selden refers to her training in Germany and Switzerland with Laban and Wigman, the European leaders of the theory and practice of the "new dance," alternately called "barefoot," "free," "absolute," and eventually "modern" dance.

Selden's books delineate basic principles of modern dance as art for two audiences—dancers and the public at large. She intends these principles to provide guidelines for anyone wishing to judge a dance composition of any time and place. Her first book is even dedicated to "the cause of study and criticism of the free dance."[2] Because so many individuals work in the new dance field, they share only a few basic theoretical principles, observes Selden. She thinks dance theory should encompass a unified terminology, an explicitly stated common set of aims, a description of basic technique, and recognized delimitations; she hopes her books will help meet these theoretical needs. She foretells continued positive development of the new dance: "With the advent of barefoot dancing, the Dance has once more advanced to the rank of an educational subject, which had not been the case for some centuries, and it will lie with the dancers themselves to establish it as an art" (*EFD*, vii). By "educational subject" she means dance is once again creative and enriching, not merely entertaining and tantalizing. She expects the forthcoming modern dance choreography will enable dance to regain the coveted status of "art."

Selden's understanding of the many parts of dance is comprehensive. She views dance as "an ideal transcending the efforts, qualities, and capacities of all dancers living and past" (*TDQ*, 4). Dance around the world, she argues, is basically the same and is guided by artistic principles which guide all the arts. The arts and dance are like a universal language with local accents in different nations. Modern dance, the art form of dance, will soon no longer be called "modern," but, she trusts, simply "dance," and will be "incontestably in possession of its rightful heritage—public interest" (*EFD*, xiii).

The Framework organizes my examination of Selden's dance theory and shows it to include almost all the topics. The majority of her ideas fit into the main categories of the *material*, the *process*, the *work*, and the *study* and *functions* of these. Though her ideas were influenced by the then current aesthetic notions, her examination of the features of dance stems from realizing the need to articulate a theoretical basis for this developing art form. Since Selden's concepts and those of Martin, H'Doubler, and Laban were source material for several aestheticians who analyzed dance, I will analyze in detail certain ideas which have been misinterpreted by some of the philosophers.

The Material

Selden highlights the special facility modern dancers have with their bodies. Body, for Selden, incorporates thought, emotion, and a person's whole being. In modern dance, Selden asserts, the dancer uses all of his or her faculties while dancing, whereas in ballet the dancer reduces the body to an infallible instrument. All the "qualities of intelligence, concentration, attention, understanding, and education" (*EFD*, 10) enter into the art. By this assertion, Selden aligns her theory with the aesthetic notion of art as a rational act, not simply a release of emotions. Selden conceptualizes mind-body unity as "body-and-soul" which leads her to define dance as "the silent language of the soul" (*EFD*, 13). Since all human beings identify with and share personal knowledge of a live human body, she thinks our body-whole being can never be abstracted or objectified by dancers or audience members, even in dancing.

Selden grants the "mind" a great part in the new dance. Her concept of mind includes thinking, feeling, and the will. Mind or consciousness creates the dance: "Movement is only beautiful as the embodiment of thought, mood, or feeling" (*TDQ*, 53). An intelligent mind, after great effort, produces brilliant creative insights. She aims these assertions against ballet and entertainment dance where choreographers merely rearrange steps, tricks, and poses while utilizing little intellectual or creative effort. In sum, for Selden, the mind's activity co-exists with the activities of the body's senses.

The kinesthetic sense is one of the dancer's prime faculties. The body, guided by the kinesthetic sense, is an "infinitely sensitive instrument" (*TDQ*, 49), because, Selden argues, it is the pathfinder in discovering new action-modes (her translation of Mary Wigman's German term *tanzerische geste*, often translated as "dance movements"). The word "movement" for Selden denotes something fixed, whereas an action-mode is not fixed, because it is not done exactly the same way with each repetition. Selden urges all arts students to study dance to sensitize and develop their kinesthetic sense, because, she claims, this sense is central to communication in all of the arts, especially the new dance. The kinesthetic sense guides discovery of new movements in modern dance: "The realm of kinesthetic exploration [is] as endless as the changing lessons of human taste" (*EFD*, 58). Dancers depend on their kinesthetic senses when improvising and performing with conviction.

Everyday movement, Selden asserts, is used as the raw material of dance similar to the way sound, color, and shape serve music, painting, and sculpture. Because the body is capable of moving in infinitely varied ways, modern dancers must choose from these variations the movements which precisely express their dance idea. An informed outlook, Selden argues, dictates the choice of movement and originates from artistic "inner necessity." Thus the material of dance, everyday movement, is on the border of dance movement, but dancers cultivate movement for its own sake and use it for artistically significant purposes.

Movement in modern dance, unlike ballet or folk dance, has no fixed steps or patterns which are arranged and re-arranged. Instead, modern dance has an infinite variety of action-modes emanating from the "intensely human character which animates the body" (EFD, 113). Action-modes include: folding-unfolding, rise-fall, press-pull, bending-reaching, rotating and twisting, undulating and heaving, swinging, swaying, and vibrating and shaking (EFD, 115-117). These action modes accent the physical orientation of modern dance movement by displaying a fluency of motion, tensional strength, muscular control, and visible use of weight. They take advantage of the three-dimensionality of the body.

Let us examine the metaphors Selden chooses to explain undulating and heaving:

> The *eternal song* of beginning and end, of rest and action. *Wave-like* motions translate the *gentle pull of life*. The stronger motions of heaving scale all the heights of *tempestuous passion*, plumb the *depths of despair and revolt*. (italics added, EFD, 116)

Many of these words—"eternal song," "gentle pull of life," "tempestuous passion," "depths of despair and revolt"—are metaphorical, emphasizing the emotional experience of undulating and heaving without giving bodily physical examples. "Wave-like," especially canonized by Isadora Duncan in her writings, refers to the many instances of waves in nature—in sound, light, and oceans. Selden expects the reader to translate this explanation into movement terms, but she does not say how to do so.

Selden explains how Laban worked out these action modes, this "grammar of motion," by at first "discarding all aesthetic considerations and delving into the more elemental regions of instinct, impulse and emotion" (TDQ, 112). She knows action modes are hard to grasp from only reading about them. One must experience them because the movements are based on the use of the weight of each body part, and they originate from the body's center. Laban called these movements weighted or "impulse" motions because they are dynamically propelled from the center of the body. In sum, quoting Laban, Selden asserts, "the dancer's principal vocabulary must be sought in motion, not emotion" (*TDQ*, 120).

In her discussion of the *material* Selden interrelates the body and the senses. As an example, she offers action-modes to show how everyday movement provides the source of many types of dance movement. Her analyses contain many analogies from nature, but only occasionally does she offer physical examples, most of which are in the glossary at the end of *Elements of the Free Dance*. In that glossary she defines terms such as "impulse," "steps," and "unfolding," though other definitions of other key words, such as "weighted," "center," and "improvisation," she omits. For readers experienced in dancing, her explanations may be useful, especially if they do the movements she suggests. For non-dancers who read her work, such as aestheticians, her explanations may not be clear because she offers so few everyday physical examples to illustrate her ideas.

Participants

When Selden uses the word "dancer" she means the creative artist as originator of dance works; the term embodies the roles of the instructor, the creator, and the performer. Though she comments about each of the roles, she concentrates on the choreographer. Dancers, like other artists, Selden observes, are born to dance. Creative joy, rhythmic sensibility, and technical fitness characterize the real dancer. Dancers are gifted individuals who are especially sensitive to line designs in relation to a "labile, shifting balance in the economy of space distribution" (*TDQ*, 126). But she thinks the ideal training for dancers must enable them to perform well technically as a means to become courageously self-expressive.

A dancer who wishes to become an artist-choreographer must work alone for two years to bring "up from the bottom of the soul the things that have not yet been" (*EFD*, 13). The dancer-artist as choreographer manipulates the elements of dance to "give the fullest and freest scope to his expression. This freedom of expression enables him to directly interpret "the stress and joy of the present, the beauty and the tenderness of the past, the promise and the visions of the future" (*EFD*, 128). In her glossary, Selden defines "choreographer" as a dance-artist who composes dances for a group. Her emphasis on a dancer's artistry and creativity obscures the fact that choreographers compose solo and group dances which are carefully worked out, practiced, staged, and repeated exactly for each performance. She does not explain the instances when choreographers teach their dances to performers who are not choreographers. While Selden assumes the dual role of dancer-choreographer is understood, she is not helpful when the roles are separate.

This lack of clarification persists in Selden's discussion of the teacher's role in training the dancer. The three references she makes to the teacher identify problems current in dance teaching practices in the 1930s. She corrects two characteristics of poor teaching: teachers must not keep students mentally dependent or indulge them in an undisciplined atmosphere. She calls for honesty among American dancers to combat the common practice of allowing people to take a few dance classes and then call themselves modern dance teachers. The teaching of technique, she reiterates, differs from teaching composition; students of modern dance require a teacher capable of teaching both. Though she hopes the situation will change, Selden fails to indicate how dancers can develop their creative capabilities when dance teaching practices are insufficient to meet the challenge.

Her view of dance teachers is mixed. Good teachers, she believes, can improve parts of the student's body which are out of proportion, such as overdeveloped muscles in the thighs and calves, but the primary role of a modern dance teacher is to train the whole personality of the dancer, not just the physical part. She thinks the university should foster high teaching standards while offering students an opportunity to study the several dimensions of dance. Among the many challenges for dance educators, she asserts, is the formulation of methods to teach the discoveries of the great dance artists. Isadora Duncan, Selden regrets, was unable to formulate her discoveries into teaching principles. Great artists are not always good teachers and may not understand how to generalize their individual aesthetic goals.

Selden touches on the interdependence and complex relationships of the three roles: dancer, choreographer, and teacher. While artists may not be the best teachers of their art, educational methodologists may offer the necessary insight into solving some of the pedagogical problems for the developing dance art. She does not acknowledge the common practice of dancers who gradually begin to choreograph and then teach other dancers to perform those dances. She also does not explain how, to earn a living, dancers often open studios and teach all who sign up for classes. For many dancers, teaching is a means to an end and not an end in itself. Granted, Selden's focus in her books is broader than teacher training; nonetheless, by leaving out these features of common practice, her explanation of the process of composing-teaching-learning is deficient.

The Process

Because modern dance looks so free, people assume its techniques are free-form and undemanding. In her essay, "The New German Credo," Selden explains how modern dance techniques use the materials of dance to train dancers to compose and perform. She explains what technique is and what it is not; technique is not the end goal of dance, as it is in ballet. Modern dancers use technique to free the body to meet the instantaneous demands for movement created from inspiration or the dance mood. Modern dance, she asserts, requires of the dancer training as rigorous as ballet. Because the training of modern dancers takes into account the whole personality, dancers experience and express technique in their own ways. Technique training addresses the dancers' minds and increases their sensitivity to the place inside the body where force and lightness meet; it therefore develops the inner and outer person. The "law of technique" enables dancers to trust the responsiveness of their bodies to embody a high artistic aim.

Selden clarifies the relationship between the training technique and the movement content of dances. Choreographers derive their techniques from specific dances they are composing at that time; the techniques are intended to train the dancers to perform those dances well. She suggests why more is known and understood about methods of training technique than about methods of composing dances: "Technique can easily be handed on," since it is the craft of dance, but the secrets of the art of composing cannot be easily "transmitted beyond the immediate future" (*TDQ*, 77). Technique, she insists, can be analyzed, but the inner truth of an artist cannot be. Selden alerts her readers to the pitfalls of perfecting dance technique: an art form has nothing more to express when its technique separates from its expressive content and becomes a finished product unto itself.

The choreographer's inner drive to express stimulates the physical activity of composing; thus the first part of composing a dance is the conception: "Although the artist finds his idea in the subconscious stratum, he must ultimately *will* it into a form sufficiently telling and permanent to embody adequately the shapeless material" (*TDQ*, 56). Selden accurately understands the creative process to involve the collaboration of all aspects of an artist's capabilities. A dance conceived only with the mind, Selden warns, is lifeless, like a stillborn infant. For example, a dance with too much mind has too much symmetry. Here she suggests criteria for a choreographer to be self-critical and for audiences and critics to see which dances are based on "inner necessity" and which are not.

Langer may have exaggerated Selden's notion that the dancer's mind inspires a dance. Selden's intention was to contrast modern dance with "mindless" ballet or entertainment dance "routines." Langer may have interpreted "conception" philosophically to mean a verbal or pre-verbal idea instead of the dance idea choreographers work out physically by using all their critical faculties.

Selden names two categories of formally structured compositions, categories which emanate from different sources. A dancer may yield entirely to his or her imagination to create space patterns or may work from a fixed theme and physically respond to an idea, a picture, or another person. These themes are dramatizations or impersonations which Selden calls "applied or illustrative dance" (*EFD*, 16). Yet even in this case, the dance message cannot be translated into words; otherwise the dance itself would be unnecessary.

Contrasting modern dance to ballet and folk dance, Selden heralds the freedom of modern dancers to create their own compositional form when they choreograph a dance. The aesthetic principles which discipline all art guide dancers in arranging their initially shapeless movements. She trusts the dancer's "innate feeling for balance, rhythm, harmonious proportion which are the general characteristics of artistic technique" (*TDQ*, 148). Techniques for composing modern dances exist, she asserts, though they are not fixed or predetermined like those of ballet. The key methods for finding expressive movements are "impulse" and "improvisation," which, she contends, serve as a constant corrective and counterbalance to rigorous technical instruction. A choreographer experiments with different impulses until finding just the right ones to express each part of the dance idea.

Selden does not explain the long and laborious process of finding each movement sequence, remembering it, connecting it to the preceding ones, perfecting it, and then moving on to the next movement sequence until the dance is complete. She only summarizes how moods or feelings guide the choreographer's selection of dance movements. Her analysis should make sense to a dancer who has repeatedly choreographed dances, but her explanation does not clarify the process in enough detail for a nondancer to fully understand it because the physical experience is difficult to put into words.

What is "good form" in dance composition? Selden claims contrast and rhythm are organic principles which guide the creation of a good dance composition. The principle of contrast has several variations. The body can make light and heavy movements whose variations provide aesthetic value to a dance and are inherent in good form. The ebb and flow of breathing is the underlying tide of life; this physiological rhythmic contrast should be taken into account when composing. The contrast between expected and surprise elements adds accent and unpredictability to a dance. Variety and repetition, she claims, are the common heritage of all the arts and basic tools for composing dances.

Rhythm, for Selden, is crucial to dance composition; it is the ordering force in all art: "Rhythm orders the relation between component parts of the dance, that is movement, rest, force, feeling, intensity, line, besides establishing the measure or wave length" (EFD, 22). Thoughtful use of rhythm contributes to a good composition, but rhythm as a concept, cautions Selden, is not to be understood as a fixed form. Selden analyzes four kinds of rhythm used in dances: musical rhythm is a feeling for measuring intervals; physical rhythm is based on breathing, life's pulse; emotional rhythm is based on the artist-dancer's oscillations of inner life, to be used with discretion, intelligence, and sincerity; and dynamic rhythm is the "crest of motion; . . . the inner tension that connects the beginning with the end of a motion" (EFD, 36). Selden's analysis of the compositional principles of modern dance breaks ground for its detail and insight by showing how to mold natural movement into expressive dances.

Selden assumes her readers realize dance is performed in a theatrical setting, on a stage with costumes, lights, and at times background sets and props, but her readers may not realize that modern dancers have a new understanding of space as "a material capable of being recreated continuously and progressively" (*TDQ*, 39). The German idea, space-body, is as substantial to a dancer as the real physical body. Selden offers one of her few physical examples in illustrating Wigman's use of space: "When she [Wigman] launches a gesture into the stage space, it seems to rebound and return to her, like a ball that she has tossed to someone; the gesture sinks back into the same inexhaustible fountain whence it was taken" (*TDQ*, 70). In the metaphor "fountain" Selden shows how Wigman's movements continuously flow and surge in, through, and with space as though it were water. Selden identifies other more physical properties of space such as direction (front, back, side, diagonal, circular), spatial patterns (designs a dancer traces), and spatial compositions derived from a sense of the three-dimensional space of the stage. She contrasts modern dance's variety of levels and directions in space with ballet's limited use of only vertical and horizontal lines. Space, Selden contends, feels to a dancer as water feels to a swimmer, a medium to penetrate and contact.

Selden examines how dance performances may employ the other arts (applied or illustrative dance, for example, draws from drama, poetry, and pantomime), and she contrasts dance with other arts to explain the unique characteristics that make it an autonomous art form. Music and dance share a rhythmic structure which serves as a direct translation of emotions. Musicians need to understand dance rhythms, for while music and dance rhythms are like each other, they are not identical. Music's rhythmic origins, she claims, are in dance, thus in modern dance musical rhythm is restored to its original home, the human body. Laban and Wigman in Europe and Doris Humphrey in the United States experimented with dance compositions without musical accompaniment to demonstrate that dance can be independent of music. Since modern dance has gained recognition and acceptance as an autonomous art, explains Selden, most choreographers use some form of musical accompaniment composed to support their dances. She identifies poetry as the other close relative of dance. Pure dance starts where music and poetry stop: "Poetry is the art of finding words—finest words—for everything that amounts to an impression, thought or emotion . . . where the powers of poetry end the opportunities of music and dance begin; they go beyond and translate indefinable emotions, impulses, reactions" (*TDQ*, 63).

Dance also shares basic materials with drama since both use the human body as an instrument. But dance, claims Selden, is not limited by language and most often expresses universal and general experience rather than specific episodes and individual feelings. Thus, although dance incorporates elements of poetry and drama, it is predominantly the art of wordless musings made visible in motion.

The outstanding features of Selden's explanation of the *process* of dance composition and performance can be distilled from the abundance of material she presents. For her, training technique is a means to an end; the end is expressive dancing. Composition is based on the universal law of materials and artistic principles of form shared by all arts. Space is both a setting and a material used in a dance. And though dance shares materials, modes of projection, and the realms of artistic creation (time, space, and mind) with other arts, dance is a unique and independent art, dependent primarily on *its* basic material, universally expressive movement of the human body.

The meaningfulness of Selden's discussion of the *process* of training, choreographing, and performing is limited to readers who are experienced in doing and seeing ballet and modern dance. She uses the terms "space" and "time" as dance jargon, giving only a few abstract non-physical examples to clarify them. Limited by her strong anti-ballet bias, she does not explain the type of freedom possible within ballet composition when she contrasts its composition methods with those of modern dance. She assumes her readers are familiar with the types of dance and the other arts to which she refers.

Observers

Selden believes the body's kinesthetic sense is the mechanism audience members rely upon for their aesthetic judgments about the dance and the dancing they see. Thanks to their kinesthetic sense, people understand the dynamic quality of a dance, along with its rhythm, order, and symmetry, because these qualities have their counterparts in everyone's body.

Movement, as a basic feature of living things, is a fundamental experience which a dance aesthetically and kinesthetically communicates from the dancer's body to the body of each member of the audience.

At times, Selden addresses the audience about dance; at other times, she addresses dancers about audiences. Since audience members more easily grasp dramatic dance than pure dance, she urges them to comprehend dance as "an art of sheer metamorphosis, of shaped time, of futurity made into a plastic present" (*TDQ*, 107). They must realize how their kinesthetic sense enables them to participate in viewing dance.

Selden reminds dancers of the diversity of an audience. Its heterogeneity requires dancers to reach beyond the individual by selecting universal emotions and truths. Since audiences will quickly stereotype a dance-artist, presentation of a wide variety of compositions can prevent an audience from forming limited expectations of an artist. Selden's analysis of the response of audience members to a modern dance concert is multilayered. Dancers, she insists, educate audiences about the art of dance by simultaneously performing, entertaining, and communicating aesthetically.

The Work

A dance is considered ephemeral because as an activity in space through time, the performance leaves no record except in the mind of the onlooker. Yet other performing arts actualize their art-communication during their performances and no one questions their existence when they are not performed. When Selden states, "Nothing short of the actual performance can convey an adequate impression of three-dimensional movement" (*TDQ*, 124), she is referring to the physical, visual, kinesthetic experience of dance which words cannot capture. The reputation of dance's ephemerality, exaggerated by Langer, may result from the lack of a widely used notation. Only once, when she cites Laban's dance script, does Selden refer to dance notation as a solution for preserving dances. Only after notation is universally used, as it is in music, she contends, will dance have a literature and no longer be perishable. Until then, each dance passes from teacher to student.

Selden's discussion of the *work*, the dance itself, interweaves the qualities of famous dances and the basic guidelines of the field. In her introduction to *The Dancer's Quest*, Selden confronts the problem of separating the dancer from the dance. She admits how difficult it is to discuss "great form" without discussing the great dancers who composed these dances, but her focus is on the aesthetic structure of their dances and not on their personalities. Talented choreographers, she acknowledges, create uniquely individual dances, but in her books she analyzes the common characteristics of these dances. Without notation, her descriptive effort must suffice as the tool of dance study. Eloquently, she identifies the aesthetic realm of a dance:

> Dance movement plays on the rim of the inexplicable, its meaning is universal-general; it is not to be read, but felt. If a story emerges all too clearly from the dance, if it could as well be expressed in words, then the dance has missed one of its main functions; that is, its dispensation in a realm where mere ecstacies of living take physical shape and thus become visible. (*TDQ*, 59-60)

Here Selden speaks from the viewpoint of a choreographer and instructs her audience to feel the physical "ecstacies" and not to read dance as they would drama or a story ballet. It is difficult to describe in words the physical experience of "mere ecstacies of living," a phrase she borrows from Laban, thus she chooses to describe the kinds of subject matter choreographers expressed in dance but none of the dynamic dance movement sequences. In *The Dancer's Quest* she analyzes with a critic's eye a few of the outstanding dances of five major choreographers, identifying their themes and styles of interpretation to illustrate the compositional range of "modern dance." These themes and styles of interpretation constitute the aesthetic goals of the choreographers.

The aesthetic goal of a dance, argues Selden, is aesthetically valid when "it transmits something universally significant" (*TDQ*, 53). This "universally significant" content in dance may be "the silent drama of the human soul" or "a plausible series of emotions," or it may "give form to experience" (*TDQ*, 69, 101, 144). A choreographer translates personal experience into a sequence of movements to which many people will respond with shared emotion.

When she turns to the aesthetic effect of a dance itself, Selden locates the impact of dance in its physical origin. The modern dancer conveys meaning through kinetic, dynamic, aesthetic, and often symbolic effects in space. Dance has an aesthetic effect which differs from the other arts. The dynamism of dance defies verbal expression. It covers the variety of energy levels dancers use to convey the physical dance images and the moving, ongoingness from its beginning to its end. Selden characterizes time in modern dance this way: "The dance wrests its existence from the future . . . . It *is* not, it is a constant becoming" (*TDQ*, 56). Dancing is the conquering of space. The action embedded in the "ing" of the words "dancing," "becoming," and "conquering" is crucial to comprehending Selden's explanation of dance dynamism. A dancer dancing is not an object fixed in time but is the vehicle that carries around the dance design while perform*ing*.

Because Selden's explanation of a dance-work is influenced by the expression-communication aesthetic theory, her discusson does not identify a dance as an entity. As a choreographer, she composes dances and therefore knows they exist when not performed, yet her written analysis of dances includes only the aesthetic intentions of choreographers and the resulting art-communication in audiences.

The Functions of the Process

The activities of composing dances and studying dance technique have educational and therapeutic value. Because the field of dance-movement therapy developed after World War II, Selden does not discuss it. She does address the issue of dance in education, focussing on how educational settings and educators treat dance-art. She holds dance educators responsible for informing lay people that dance is an art, not just a physical, recreational activity to be done correctly. The spirituality or high aesthetic goal of dance, she contends, is the emphasis in the American colleges and universities where dance is taught. Yet she sees this spirituality as a particularly American distortion of the total dance process. In contrast, in European studios modern dance is used to liberate "physical ecstacies" neglected during the Victorian era (*TDQ*, 180). Dance educators are responsible for teaching all sides of dance—physical, cognitive, emotional, and spiritual—without emphasizing one part over another.

Selden's treatment of *The Functions of the Process* is addressed to people familiar with the issues within the field and includes useful examples. She offers an impassioned plea for solutions to the problems of preserving and developing the art of dance. Her interest in a sound educational context for dance is characteristic of her broad perspective.

The Functions of the Work

To clarify how modern dance functions in its contemporary context Selden examines how ballet and folk dance fit their historical and cultural contexts. When she explains the functions and the relationships among folk, ballroom, and art dance forms she gives no examples, assuming her readers are familiar with them. She does provide her readers with valuable insight into them: folk, ballroom, and ballet share fixed forms; that is, they have "steps" which evolved and are elaborated upon by convention. She explains how ballet was the art dance of the seventeenth century when choreographers evolved fixed steps in performances unified around a plot. The types of dance which are guided by cultural and social conventions she calls formal. All these forms arose from communal dance and share "the common wish for entertainment, recreation" (*EFD*, 75). While she explains the origins and purposes of folk, ballet, and national dance in her discussion of *The Functions of the Work*, Selden does not adequately differentiate between the works of dance used for social purposes and the processes of composing them.

The Work Studied

Though Selden does not delve deeply into dance history, ethnography, or sociology, she refers to basic issues in these fields. She does explore in depth the cultural context of dance in twentieth-century Europe and especially in America, focussing on how contemporary dance, like the other arts, emerges from and speaks for the historical time in which we live. Art is a valuable cultural storehouse of human experiences where the past and present intersect. Dance, she insists, reflects how people view themselves in each period of history.

Features of modern dance reflect contemporary times: discord, harmony, and tension. Selden cites, as an illustration, the subject matter of Humphrey's dances. Because they range widely in twentieth-century topics, including psychological needs, wonders of nature, problems of poverty and wealth, and family and women's issues, her dances speak to the imagination of contemporary audiences.

Selden analyzes how modern dance reflects the contemporary preoccupation with the passion for emotional release and the need to mechanically control energy. It contains nervous and taut line designs and movements, and rhythms which feel charged with the need to break loose and to achieve definite objectives.

Selden's Language

How clearly do Selden's ideas explain the major dimensions of dance? Selden's theoretical consideration of dance is thorough and includes almost all of the topics in our Framework of Topics Intrinsic to Dance Theory. Her understanding of dance stems from direct experience and represents the reality of the art in the 1930s. The major drawback in her work lies in a minor feature of her writing. While the examples used to clarify her terms work effectively for people who have experience in dance, these metaphorical expressions were not sufficiently clear to people without dance experience, as is evident in the incomplete understanding and inaccurate interpretation of her ideas by the aestheticians. The gap between dance-based experience, so dear to Selden, and philosophical abstraction, so dear to aestheticians, could not be bridged by Selden's metaphorical language.

NOTES

1 Elizabeth Selden, *Elements of the Free Dance* (New York: A. S. Barnes, 1930), xv. Further page references in this chapter to this book will be cited parenthetically in the text preceded by *EFD*.

2 Selden, *The Dancer's Quest* (Berkeley: University of California Press, 1935), xiii. Further page references in this chapter to this book will be cited parenthetically in the text preceded by *TDQ*.

6

THE DANCE THEORY OF
JOHN MARTIN

In 1927 John Martin (1893–1985) became one of the first full-time dance critics for a major American newspaper. Writing for the *New York Times*, he championed the newly emerging modern dance and he wrote many books on the broad field of dance. After retiring from this position in 1965, he became an adjunct professor of dance at the University of California, Los Angeles.

Four of Martin's books—*The Modern Dance* (1933), *America Dancing* (1936), *Introduction to the Dance* (1939), and *The Dance: The Story of the Dance Told in Pictures and Text* (1946)—will be considered here. Though none of his books includes a bibliography, the scope of his discussions suggests he read widely in aesthetics, history, theater, art, architecture, and dance. Yet he refers to only a few of the authors who influenced his thinking, such as Havelock Ellis, Jane Harrison, Theodor Lipps, and Rudolf Laban. His ideas and writing style reflect other influences, especially from aesthetics and psychoanalysis.

Although Martin includes all dimensions of the field of dance in his books, his primary focus is the new modern dance. Between 1930 and 1940, he conducted a series of lecture demonstrations on modern dance at the New School of Social Research in New York City. Four of these lectures given in 1931-1932 are collected in *The Modern Dance*.

In the four books, Martin places modern dance within the context of other forms and functions of dance, but his overriding purpose is to explain dance as an art to the public and to help dancers clarify their thinking about dance. He identifies three principles all forms of dance share: movement is their basic material, kinesthetic empathy is their way of communicating, and the human body moving rhythmically is their goal. This theoretical understanding of dance, he predicts, will help the field to grow and prosper.

Martin believes dance is as fundamental to a person's life as diges-
tion is to the living body. Dance is basic to our nature because movement is
the medium in which we live. All dance forms result from strong emo-
tional-physical responses to deep and stirring life experiences. He gives as
examples jumping for joy, pacing in worry, and trembling with fear. A
wide variety of dancers evolved an equally wide variety of dances because
dance can convey internal and emotional reactions too deep to express in
words. This common need to resort to movement to express emotional
states is what Martin identifies as "basic dance."[1] Human beings need to
dance, and all forms and functions of dance stem from basic dance.

The Material

Martin interrelates the topics of the *material* of dance. For example
he says, "The dance exists exclusively in terms of the movement of the
body, not only in the obvious sense that the dancer moves, but also in the
less apparent sense that the spectator's response is likewise a matter of
body movement."[2] Here Martin identifies the kinesthetic sense—the
muscle memory each person has—as the mechanism guiding dancing and
the receptivity of observers to dance. The body, moving, serves human life
internally and externally:

> [Bodily movement] is the most elementary physical experience
> of human life. Not only is it found in the vital functional
> movement of the pulse and throughout the body in its business
> of keeping alive but it is also found in the expression of all
> emotional experiences . . . . The body is the mirror of all
> thought.[3]

Here, Martin identifies the pivotal role movement plays in our lives and
presents the interrelated visceral, emotional, and rational capabilities as
coequal.

In each of his books, Martin details how the kinesthetic sense oper-
ates in daily life. He speaks of "inner mimicry" or "muscle sympathy" to
show how a person's response to a dance is as natural as any other daily
kinesthetic response, such as seeing a tall building or noticing someone
yawn. Dancers express emotional and mental experiences "through the
irrational medium of bodily movement" (*MD*, 10). Martin does not use

"irrational medium" in a pejorative sense. He argues against the tyranny of words and their "academic" prestige, while urging members of the audience to respond to dance with their nonrational capabilities. The body and its movement, he points out, are the means of making dance and receiving its communication.

The primary contribution of modern dance to dance history, Martin asserts, is the discovery of movement as the actual substance of the dance. Pose, position, or musical interpretation were previously central to dance. Now movement alone is the medium for conveying aesthetic and emotional content from one individual's consciousness to another's. The modern dancer feels "emotional experience can express itself through movement directly" (MD, 18). Movement antedates language and is the first means of communicating ideas between people. Such communication, claims Martin, is universal: though people do not speak the same language, they move in similar ways and for similar reasons.

When a dancer composes a dance, Martin contends, he or she selects movements from the myriad movements of daily life. All movement can potentially convey human intention. The dancer's selection of movements is based on a combination of personal, rational, emotional, and aesthetic needs. Dancers combine their mind, kinesthetic sense, and other senses in making a dance. This holistic response in dance is natural: "There is no experience of one's emotional life which is without its motor concomitants, and it is quite possible to recall and in a degree reproduce certain emotional states or experiences by a repetition of movements which are associated with them" (AD, 113). Martin borrows these ideas from Theodor Lipps's theory of kinesthetic empathy[4] to cap his explanation of how dancers use bodily movement in dance to convey the aesthetic content of a dance directly to an audience.

Choreographers, Martin asserts, make everyday movement into dance by amplifying the ongoing dynamic quality of a sequence of movements. Dance movement "contains no static elements" (MD, 31). To strengthen this idea Martin introduces Laban's idea of movement as the ebb and flow of energy between the extremes of complete relaxation and complete tension. In other words, no movement actually stops, though momentary rests punctuate dance movement sequences and add rhythmic texture to them. Muscular rhythm, Martin thinks, regulates the energy or force of dance movement and controls its dynamic flow.

In sum, the body's senses and intellect, everyday movement, and dance movement work in concert. In his descriptions of everyday movement Martin gives physical examples and then generalizes about how a dancer chooses among these movements to make a dance.

Though Martin's choice of words demonstrates his sensitivity to the need to correct the popular notion of mind-body separation, he nonetheless divides their functions when he refers to the mind as the rational or intellectual capability and the body as the dancer's instrument. He is unaware of this hidden contradiction. Is "body" the part of a person below his or her head, or does "body" refer to the total person, the entire physical body and personality? Martin repeatedly refers to society's sense of the "vile" body, though he hopes the appreciation of "body" is changing. Yet in his references to the body as the dancer's instrument, he claims dancers objectify their bodies when they use them to dance. This implies a hierarchy of the aesthetic criteria of the mind over the body and has the ring of "mind over matter."

Participants

In discussing the roles of the people directly involved in dance, Martin uses the term "modern dancer" to mean choreographer. The aim of modern dance training is to enable dancers to become choreographers. Indeed, that idea was generally accepted in the field of modern dance, whereas in ballet only a few dancers become choreographers. Martin does not write about the role of the teacher in the context of choreographing and performing, though he makes valuable points about teaching in the context of dance education.

The Process

> Be cautious when you use the word "technique," for unless you specify otherwise, you are including a great deal; you are including three techniques which are to be found in the practise of any art. They are the technique of the instrument, the technique of the medium and the technique of form. (MD, 88)

Here Martin shows astute understanding of the complexity of the meaning of dance "technique" and identifies a potentially confusing issue for dancers and non-dancers alike because "technique" is dance jargon. He defines technique as simply the way something is done but then points out how training ("the instrument"), composing ("the form"), and performing ("the medium") each require highly specialized techniques.

Dancers continuously study techniques of the instrument to develop almost "a super-body by reason of its strength, its control, its plasticity, and its ability to respond instantaneously to demands made upon it."[5] A highly trained and responsive body, Martin argues, is advantageous for communicating dance ideas, but a good technician is not necessarily a good artist. Technique should not be an end in itself but only a method to bring about the end result of dance as art. Like Selden, Martin thinks ballet makes the presentation of technical perfection the goal of ballet-art, while modern dance uses technical body training as a means for the dancer to express emotional content via dance movement. Martin repeatedly warns the followers of modern dance pioneers not to crystallize their technique-practice methods into technical systems; the resulting crystallization would ultimately recreate the expressionless spectacle of ballet. Martin's analysis highlights the interdependence of training technique with the other techniques of choreographing and performing.

Performance is the central function of art dance. Only in performance, when an audience is present, Martin believes, is form necessary for dance. Composition is the giving of "form" to movement sequence; thus modern dance choreographers shape movement through space, in time, and with dynamics to form emotionally expressive dances; expression is their primary goal. Choreographers, according to Martin, select ideas from their life experience which they then abstract to illuminate essential and universal messages. Human beings, he thinks, intuitively give phenomena form by fitting parts together in a satisfying order: "This fitting together of parts constitutes what may be called the internal form of composition" (MD, 88-89).

Martin examines how a choreographer masters the movement selection process. Dancers use creative intelligence to select from their large movement vocabulary the movements they will work with. The rest, for the moment, are of no value. A dancer "must select the kind of movement that is not subordinate and subsidiary to physical necessity, but is the product of a mental, an emotional, a non-physical demand" (*MD*, 87). This "mental, emotional, non-physical demand" motivates a dancer to compose a dance.

Rhythm guides this process of fitting dance movements together. Martin offers one of his few physical examples to explain how coordinated movement has intrinsic rhythmic content. He points out how our arms automatically extend to assist our bodies when we are about to lose our balance. Modern dancers build on this naturally occurring rhythmic accent in the upper body to make their standing and falling movements more exciting to watch: "When these movements have been arranged in rhythmic relation to each other, the arrangement dictated still by the logic of the inner feeling but at the same time productive of an aesthetic reaction in an onlooker, the composition is complete" (*MD*, 60). For Martin, form is the unifying process of all art: "only form produces aesthetic response" (*MD*, 68).

Martin claims modern dance is "virtually free from predetermined forms" (*ID*, 76) but suggests all compositions have four components: time, space, dynamism, and metakinesis. In practice, these factors are inseparable; only in a theoretical discussion is it possible to identify and analyze these parts. Martin examines how each factor is used in composing a dance. "Time" is periodicity, accent, and unaccent. The muscle rhythm which dictates this time dimension of movement is an integral part of the movement phrase and therefore helps produce the dynamic quality of movement in space.

The awareness and use of space, claims Martin, is a major contribution made by modern dance to theater dance. Dancers not only move in and through space but consciously relate to it as an environment with physical properties and emotional overtones. Space in dance terminology means more than air or the space around something. Laban and Wigman, Martin explains, understood space as a medium for dance, as water is for a fish, or air is for a bird—to engage, to contend with, or to shape. A sphere of space encases the body, in which and with which the body moves.

The third component of a dance, dynamism, means the continuous flow of movement along with the quality or intensity with which movements are made—soft, firm, flowing, tense, percussive. Muscle tone controls these dynamic variations which are modulated until the dance is over.

Metakinesis, the last component of a dance, draws on "the implications of mood, purpose, function and emotion" carried within any movement (*ID*, 62). Dancers improvise to find the exact movement which will authentically express the internal state about which they are dancing. Each movement then is designed to fit the expressive purpose of the dance.

Modern dance choreographers, Martin argues, do not use a set of predesigned steps. This is why Martin repeatedly defines modern dance as a point of view rather than a technique system. Artists freely derive their own techniques and compositional forms for each dance from their personal inner aesthetic and expressive necessity.

Dance has not been understood as an independent art, Martin believes, because it has been associated in its productions with poetry in drama and music in opera. Martin pries the various arts apart while showing how they are related. Like Selden and H'Doubler, he embraces the common assumption of dance as the first art. Dance, music, poetry, and drama, he claims, emerged as individual arts from their common origin in religious ritual, yielding shared features and goals. He thinks that just as "basic" dance exists, "basic" music also exists. In their "basic" functions, music and dance are inseparable. While as art they aim to communicate, their different materials produce unique results: the harmonic melodic sound of music; the ordered, patterned words of poetry; the individuated life-revealing action of drama; and the universally expressive, aesthetically ordered movements of dance.

Modern dance, a composite art, grows and changes, reflecting contemporary times. In the early days of modern dance, Duncan used music to stimulate her dances, but modern dance choreographers now consider music of secondary importance. Whenever possible music is composed specifically for a dance and performed as its support. Like architecture, dance movement molds the three-dimensional space in which it occurs. And like pantomime, some dance movements depict literal and specific meanings.

Martin believes modern dance is guided by the principles of "modernism" in the arts. Since the advent of technological recording devices such as film, the goal of contemporary artists is no longer to reproduce nature. The modern arts depend on individual interpretation, personal selection, and unique presentation. In this modern mode of working, artists value distortion, idealization, and abstraction. Modern dances have these features, and thus may be characterized as "modern."

In Martin's discussion of the *process* of dance, his ideas remain broad generalizations because he offers only a few examples. On the other hand, he clarifies complex issues about the processes of dancing when he both separates and interrelates the techniques for training, composing, and performing. The reasons Martin gives for how settings affect the functions of dance elucidate the performance and theatrical characteristics of dance, and Martin untangles the intertwining relationships among the several arts. But he does this in too general and abstract a manner and assumes readers are familiar with the artists, the arts, and the cultural contexts of the art activities to which he refers. Therefore, Martin's writing cannot make the art of dance clear if readers have not had first-hand experience with techniques of the art, the work involved in creating a work of art, and the many factors combined in the production of performing art. He does not enlighten those who are not already enlightened.

Observers

People intuitively respond to any art, not just dance, Martin argues, with all their bodily senses in conjunction with their intellect. An aesthetic experience occurs when we perceive, not simply "understand or see," something in a way we have never perceived it before and appreciate it in a new way. Agreeing with Selden, Martin holds that the daily familiarity of people with bodily movement prevents any movement from being entirely abstract—divorced from behavior—or non-representational because the human body itself is producing the movement.

Martin is sensitive to the interdependence of artists, audiences, and critics for box office results. His newspaper articles significantly promoted the new field of modern dance as an autonomous art in America in the 1930s and 1940s. Because too few choreographers notate their dances, he laments, much dance history is lost, and, thererore, much theoretical analysis depends on what critics say: how they see, how they respond to, and how they write about dance in their newspaper and magazine columns. The writings of critics, according to Martin, serve as the major source for dance historians.

The Work

Martin interprets the value of dance in terms of the expression-communication theory of art popularized by Collingwood and Langer. In art, he asserts: "one individual conveys from his consciousness to that of another individual a concept which transcends his powers of rational statement" (*MD*, 35). Using words similar to these—"expression," "concept," "transcends an individual's power," and "rational"—Martin defines dance: "The dance is the expression, by means of bodily movements arranged in significant form, of concepts which transcend the individual's power to express by rational and intellectual means" (*MD*, 84). These statements are found in Martin's earliest book, *The Modern Dance*. Seven years later, in *Introduction to the Dance*, he broadens his explanation of art-making to encompass the Freudian view of art as a compensatory process, where the imagination makes up for whatever a human being cannot have, achieve, or create in day-to-day life. Though Martin changes his understanding of why people make art, all his descriptions of works of art emphasize the communication process between artist and audience. In each book he analyzes the aesthetic intentions in the work of major dance artists, focussing on their creative emphases, virtuoso communication skills, and emotional expression.

In spite of his emphasis on the expressive function of a dance, Martin does identify a dance as a distinct entity, separate from the choreographer's intention to communicate and from the dancer's expression of this intention. Because he is a critic, Martin takes the non-ephemeral existence of a dance for granted. He refers to a "dance" as a work of art, in one instance, when he describes the difficulty choreographers have retaining the spontaneity of their personal, kinetic, emotional experience in a formed dance-work which can be repeated in a series of performances. He again refers to a dance as an entity separate from its communication in comparison to drama, in relation to other modern arts, in his discussion of movement as a unified substance, and in his discussion of a great choreographer's independent works of art.

In brief, Martin thinks universal emotional associations, translated into action and ordered into an organic form, convey the artist's aesthetic intention. When responding to the artist's intention, audience members need only be receptive with their "mechanisms of inner mimicry, motor response and association" (*ID*, 57). The artist's intention need not be exactly grasped by the audience for the artist's aesthetic communication to be successful.

Martin calls dance an illiterate art, and he hopes that in time Labanotation, Laban's notation system, will overcome that illiteracy. The lack of notation, Martin points out, is a major reason for the lack of repertoire: like music, dance might have fallen back on its past to maintain quality performances during periods of low creativity. Notation, Martin argues, will greatly aid theorizing. He writes sarcastically:

> Music with its method of notation and its elaborate fabrications of systems and codes, can be indulged by the academicians under the midnight oil; it is reducible to paper and ink, those noble instruments of literacy; it makes appeal to that loftiest of lofties, the scholar's theorizing intellect. The dance, poor wretch, handed down from generation to generation by imitation, if at all, illiterate, unrecordable, depends for its existence upon the vulgar exertions of the body, that vile prison in which the sin of Adam has encased man's spirit. (*AD*, 94)

Martin's biting comments mourn the lowly, unrefined status of dance caused by Victorian prejudices against the central role of the body in dance. Without written records, dance has not yet lifted itself to the lofty rank of a fine art.

Martin is a strong advocate for the illiterate field which he is struggling to make more literate. His writing reveals the aesthetic intentions of artists, gleaned from what they say about their purposes. As a critic he shows his audience how to enjoy the non-verbal communication of the dances he expertly analyzes.

The Functions of the Process

Like Selden, Martin hopes dance will contribute to individuals and our culture as a whole by fostering a positive attitude toward the body. In

Introduction to the Dance, he devotes a chapter to the topic of education. Dance in education furthers the progressive educational goal of interrelating the intellectual, emotional, and physical growth of a student. Dance composition achieves this educational goal: "It functions . . . in terms not of pure intellection but of applied intellection, as a link between feeling and action" (*ID*, 291).

Educators, Martin argues, must differentiate the professional goal of training performers from the educational goal of using dance to increase the creative capabilities and physical expressiveness of students. In his discussion of "professionalism" in relation to dance education, he gives educators three charges: they should instruct professional artists about teaching, apply the art and science of education to the teaching methods of dance technique and composition, and prevent the development of inflexible technique systems. Regrettably, he offers no examples to illustrate these problems. He does not view dance in education as a form of therapy; instead, he believes it is a basic art experience in which all human beings are entitled to participate.

Functions of the Work

Martin identifies the different functions of several dance forms: art dance is for communication; folk and social dance are for play and recreation; erotic dance is for courtship; and spectacular dance is for entertainment. Hence, the setting and purpose of a dance determine if it is an artistic performance. In religious ritual, the dancer's audience are the gods and spirits. In the social settings of folk and ballroom dance, the groups or partners dance for themselves or each other. And in a theatrical setting, the purpose may be to display skill or express a universal reality in an aesthetic form created by the individual artist. When a dance performance is "spectacular," in the ballet style of the 1930s, Martin, like Collingwood, thinks the audience responds objectively and is entertained; when a performance is designed for the audience to participate in subjectively and vicariously, it functions as art.

Martin regards the play aspect of recreational dancing as a valuable human activity, and as is his bent, interrelates these functions of dance: "What remains to us of recreational dancing is comprised in the so-called ballroom dance, which is erotic; the revived dancing of folk dances which is convivial and gregarious; and the many but still unorganized layman's approaches to the dance, which are essentially creative" (*ID*, 145). Though in describing non-technological societies, Martin uses "simple," a term common in the 1920s, his outdated terminology does not lessen the value of his observations, especially when he analyzes the social function of recreational, ritual-religious, and entertainment forms of dance. Recreational dances, he agrees with Selden, can be grouped into three categories: dances of play, dances of magic and religion, and dances for the release of tension. Dance in these "simple" societies, Martin points out, is integrated into their social workings, not isolated as an "art" as in our society.

Martin gives examples of social and folk dances to reassure readers of their familiarity with these dances. Ritual, folk, social, and entertainment dance have fixed forms with set steps. Because dancers and audiences share common knowledge of these dances, the product binds them together. They share in the repeated performance of the dance but rarely in the process of creating it as do participants in dance therapy or in creative dance in educational settings. Choreographers of art dance forms, Martin explains, use movements from ritual, social, folk, and entertainment forms of dance in their choreography. These movements enrich a dance's meaning for artist and audience alike because the dances are community property from a common cultural non-verbal heritage.

The Material Studied

Martin does not mention kinesiology by name, but in *American Dancing* and *Introduction to the Dance*, he shows keen awareness of research in this field and in the related field of physical therapy. In *America Dancing* Martin discusses Bird Larson, the first dancer to study and teach physical therapy applied to dance, and he mentions the noteworthy work of Mabel Ellsworth Todd, the teacher of anatomy and correctives at Columbia University Teachers College where Bird Larson studied and taught in the mid 1920s. In his explanation of "movement sense" in *Introduction to the Dance*, Martin defines the kinesthetic sense:

> Sense organs are to be found in the tissue of the muscles and in the joints, which respond to movements of the body in much the same way that the eye responds to light or the ear to sound. . . . They register change of posture however small

throughout the body, and thus tend to keep it always in alignment, so to speak. (*ID*, 43)

Martin's knowledge of kinesiology characterizes the breadth and mastery of his scholary range; he reaches into other arts to amplify his explanation of human kinesthesia. He accurately foresees the applicability of information from the fields of kinesiology and physical therapy to dance theory and practice.

The Work Studied

In his comprehensive overview of dance history, Martin adopts Havelock Ellis's notion that periods in dance history emphasize either expression of the art's messages, "Romantic" periods, or virtuoso achievements of the artist's skills, "Classical" periods.[6] Martin reviews in detail the varied uses of the terms "Romantic" and "Classical" and traces these styles through dance history. Art products, in Martin's view, result from the response of artists to their environment. He applies his compensatory theory of art to the cultural climate in historical periods. Martin's understanding of the history of the arts cuts across the academic subjects of history, anthropology, and sociology. The changes in dance from one period in history to another, he argues, are merely variations of style. Whether as crystallization of technique, subject matter, or choreographic form, "style" for Martin is influenced by geography, cultural climate, and nation of origin, and it applies to collective and personal ways of dancing.

Since dance historians have minimal direct evidence from notated scores of dances from the past, Martin identifies the types of external evidence on which dance history depends. Using an analogy to music, he illustrates the dilemma the lack of dance notation has caused: where would music be now if it were reconstructed from the memories of old musicians or newspaper reports by critics of the period?

Martin's Language

Martin's goal in writing his theoretical books was to clarify dance for the audience and to teach them how to "understand" dance kinesthetically. To meet this challenge, he must choose his words precisely. He gives examples from daily life to bring his readers close to the non-verbal issues he addresses. Two interdependent problems arise in his choice of words.

In the first place, he uses the words "movement," "body," and "dance" as jargon, in an overly limited, referential way. Jargon evolves in any field, but readers outside the field may not understand the meaning of these basic words. Martin assumes his readers have dance experience. Because Martin did not define all his terms, the aestheticians who read his books did not comprehend the physical complexities in his words. A look at the word "movement" will reveal this overly general quality of Martin's writing.

Is a "movement" a skip—meaning step and hop on the right foot and then step and hop on the left foot—or a blink of an eyelid, or both? Though Martin distinguishes dance movement from such daily movements as expanding and contracting the lungs or kicking a football, he characterizes a dance movement only as a dynamic series of motions with no static action. Yet he does not give examples to illustrate how a dancer makes an everyday movement dynamic.

In the second place, Martin gives too few dance examples when he explains how movements are used in a dance; therefore, his discussions remain too general. Even when Martin offers examples, some do not support his assertions. For instance, he explains how Doris Humphrey teaches specific techniques of dance composition to her students but never uses them herself because she always works directly with the movement idea itself. This apparent contradiction may confuse readers about how a choreographer goes about ordering dance ideas into a formal structure. Theodore Meyer Greene (see Chapter 8), who quoted extensively from Martin's books, concluded modern dancers have no formal method of composing their dances. Aware that his words might be confusing, Martin recommends attending performances, composing dances, and above all dancing. Experience, he asserts, is far superior to analysis and theory for genuine understanding.

Martin's audience viewpoint contributes to what may be termed an outsider's picture of the physical dance experience. In writing about dance, Martin's words are often non-physical. The precedence his theoretical explanation gives to the communication process over the dance itself may be the primary reason why, in the final analysis, non-dancers find it difficult to understand what a *dance* is after reading his books. Had his terms been more physically oriented, readers with little experience in

dancing would more readily grasp his astute analysis of the interrelation-
ship among the functions, styles, and creative processes of dance.

NOTES

[1] John Martin, *The Dance: The Story of the Dance Told in Pictures and Text* (New York: Tudor Publishing Company, 1946), 6-17.

[2] John Martin, *America Dancing* (New York: Dodge Publishing Company, 1936), 107. Further page references to this book will be indicated parenthetically in the text preceded by *AD*.

[3] John Martin, *The Modern Dance* (1933; rpt. Brooklyn, N.Y.: Dance Horizons Press, 1965), 8. Further page references to this book will be signalled parenthetically in the text preceded by *MD*.

[4] Theodor Lipps, *Psychological Studies*, tr. Herbert C. Sanborn (Baltimore: Williams and Wilkins, Co., 1926).

[5] John Martin, *Introduction to the Dance* (1939; rpt. Brooklyn, N.Y.: Dance Horizons Press, 1965), 271. Further page references to this work will be indicated parenthetically in the text preceded by *ID*.

[6] A detailed analysis of Havelock Ellis's chapter on dance in his *Dance of Life* (Boston: Houghton Mifflin, 1923) appears in Judith B. Alter, "Sleuthing Havelock Ellis's Essay 'The Art of Dancing,'" in *Conference Proceedings 1985* of the Society of Dance History Scholars (Riverside, Calif.: University of California, Riverside, Dance Department, 1985).

7

THE DANCE THEORY OF
MARGARET H'DOUBLER

Margaret H'Doubler (1889–1984) was a dance educator and master teacher. In 1927, while teaching at the University of Wisconsin, she initiated the first college-level degree program in dance in the United States. In her two manuals on teaching dance, written in 1921 and 1925, she instructs choreographers how to use music visualization to compose dances for the pageants, popular in the first quarter of this century.[1] By 1940, in her most widely circulated book, she identified dance as a completely autonomous art, independent of music.[2] She wrote this book, *Dance: A Creative Art Experience*, "to set forth a theory and philosophy that will help us see dance scientifically as well as artistically." [3] H'Doubler assumes scientific analysis can enhance the understanding and creating of art dance. She focusses on universal qualities and conditions of dance, not on individual dances and dancers. Addressing teachers, lay people, and dancers, she examines the overall field of dance. In this book, analyzed here, the range of the topics she discusses goes beyond her earlier books and incorporates most of topics in the Framework of Topics Intrinsic to Dance Theory.

H'Doubler's extensive annotated bibliography contains 198 entries arranged into six categories: background reading primarily from aesthetics; material directly related to dance and dancers; only five entries about dance script; twenty-eight entries about rhythm, music, and dance accompaniment; bibliographies; and periodicals. Among her many enthusiastic annotations are emphatic recommendations for the books of Selden and Martin. Indeed, the words H'Doubler uses to explain many of the topics in *Dance: A Creative Art Experience* are quite similar to those of Selden and Martin. Judith Anne Gray reveals that H'Doubler's informal style of scholarship often led her to borrow ideas and words from her favorite philosophers as well.[4]

The Material

In her examination of the *material* of dance H'Doubler blends a holistic, even spiritual, approach with her scientific analysis derived from biology and kinesiology. The body, H'Doubler claims, "should be considered as the outer aspect of personality, for it is the agent through which we receive impressions from the external world and by which we communicate our meaning" (63). As the art of the whole person, dance employs the body as well as the mind by encompassing the dancer's emotional, intellectual, spiritual, and physical capabilities. In a note, H'Doubler corrects the misleading dichotomy of mind and body. Although they are not separate, she explains, the phrase "mind and body" is a convenient way to talk about the different functions of a person. The aestheticians who read her words overlooked this disclaimer and continued to employ that distorted description of a human being. In agreement with Selden and Martin, she concludes that the body presents the whole personality.

H'Doubler highlights the role of the kinesthetic sense, though the standard senses (touch, taste, sight, smell, and hearing), she acknowledges, are commonly thought to be the body's primary way of responding to external and internal stimuli. The kinesthetic sense reports to the mind "the exact state of muscular contraction, the range of joint movement, and the tensions of the tendons in any movement" (72). Even though she falls back upon "mind-body" terminology, H'Doubler stresses the unifying function of the kinesthetic sense. It provides information from within our bodies, enabling us to judge the timing, force, and extent of our movements and to make appropriate physical-mental adjustments. The kinesthetic sense, she concludes, provides the channel that integrates inner and outer experience.

Random everyday movement, H'Doubler asserts, provides the source material for a dance. Any of these movements, which express internal emotional states, are the artistic seeds of expressive, meaningful dance movements. For H'Doubler, dance movement should be as natural as possible, meaning dancers should adopt unstylized and unformalized gestures and actions: walk, run, skip, hop, jump, leap, gallop, and slide. All dance movements are variations of these universal and everyday locomotor activities.

H'Doubler's detailed discussion of everyday movement as the source of dance movement offers many physical examples of movements. All movement in dance or daily activity shares basic features. Movement can be executed with high tension, complete relaxation, or any amount of intensity between these extremes. These modulations of energy create the "qualities" movements can have. Especially effective in making a dance are such qualities as swinging, percussive, sustained, and collapsing. She identifies the modulated use of tension as the basis for aesthetic experience and expression in dance movement because tension produces a heightened sensitivity and awareness in the dancer and the audience.

Rhythm also differentiates dance movement from daily movement: rhythm is "the primary, fundamental art form; its study is essential to all art, but especially to dance because of the latter's kinesthetic basis of perception" (85). Repetition, a part of rhythm, inheres in the function of muscle and nerve. When movement is done consciously and used intentionally as an aesthetic tool, expressive movement becomes art.

H'Doubler's comments about the *material* of dance are scattered throughout her book. She connects body-mind-spirit, explaining how the kinesthetic sense binds the personality together and acts as a conduit for receiving and expressing non-verbal information. Her physical sense of the body makes her arguments persuasive but not entirely clear to non-dancers because the mind-body dichotomy pervades her analysis.

Participants

In H'Doubler's view, dancer means choreographer. The basic pleasure of moving motivates the dancer to make dance art. The motor sensitivity, unique personality and daily experiences of the dancer are the sources of a choreographer's creative abilities, enabling that person to transform everyday movements into organized sequences and finished dances. (Her discussion of the teacher's role in dance education is analyzed under the heading *The Functions of the Process* below.)

The Process

Because H'Doubler wrote her book to convince her colleagues in higher education of the academic value of dance activity, she leaves performance out of her analysis of the *process*. Her examination of technique and composition in relation to the other arts highlights the intellectual, emotional, and social benefits students gain from dance experience. Like Martin, H'Doubler thinks of technique as both a mental-creative and a physical-mechanical process "which enables the dancer to embody aesthetic experience in a composition, as well as the skill to execute it" (147). Systematic body training, for H'Doubler, is not a complete method of instruction but is needed for moving efficiently. This training develops a discriminating kinesthetic sense to control motor technique. When the movements can be repeated automatically, she asserts, the mind is freed for creative activity. Motor technique must be neither purely imitative, repeated in a rote manner, nor a collection of arbitrary skills or feats. Technique must adhere to anatomical, physiological, and psychological principles.

H'Doubler insists that technique of training and composition must be more than just a collection of arbitrary skills. Training technique should be taught so students achieve a personal level of performance which supersedes the mere imitation of someone else's techniques and enables the dancer's mind to control the body's natural tendencies. In composing dances, a dancer should have experience with and select from a wide range of movement.

As with Selden and Martin, H'Doubler's focus on the natural quality of dance technique reflects her anti-ballet stance. Technique training must change untrained, natural movement patterns into viable material for art. Technique is a physical activity, and from her biological perspective, H'Doubler offers a condensed definition of it: "Technique of the physical instrument is the motor intelligence . . . . Dance technique is the dancer's artistic integrity working through his nerves and muscles" (91). In sum, dance technique helps achieve a combined educational, artistic, and physical goal.

Movements become a dance after they are arranged in a form that allows their meaning to show. All the arts, including dance, she argues, have as their common source the fundamental human need of revealing the inner life in an external pattern. H'Doubler, like the other modern dance exponents, advocated a dance form not codified in a way similar to ballet because a predictable technique form limits expression.

Thus the technique of dance composition "transforms experience into the form of its expression" (67). H'Doubler devotes four of the nine chapters in her book to dance composition. Her chapter titles—"Form as Organic Unity," "Form and Content," "Form and Structure," and "Dance and Music"—suggest the scope of her concern and the abstract manner in which she discusses the topic. She prefaces her account of dance composition by discussing the nature of art. Yrjo Hirn and John Dewey strongly influenced her thinking about art and the process of creating it.[5] H'Doubler accepts Hirn's theory of art as a process occurring in developmental stages. She divides the dancer's composition process into the vital and exuberant release stage, the organizing stage, and the mature stage of the mind's expression. She accepts Dewey's basic premise of art as experience, a rhythmic intaking and outgoing in which everyone can engage. The very title of H'Doubler's book, *Dance: A Creative Art Experience*, adapts the title of Dewey's *Art as Experience*.

Echoing Dewey, H'Doubler believes the fusion of inner and outer experience produces the fullest meaning in an art form. This form is achieved in dance when movement is emotionally charged and intellectually disciplined: "If inner and outer rhythm are one, communication is rich and complete; if not, the dance is likely to be too physical, too much of the body, rather than of the mind through the body" (87). The creative process for H'Doubler requires the mind's expressive faculty to organize the motor and emotional impulses.

She articulates the steps a choreographer follows in making a dance. The first step is when the dancer feels the need to make a dance; there must be something to dance about. The ideas, impressions, or psychic images to "dance about" have a physical manifestation and must be organized to show inner meaning. This unifying of inner and outer elements, H'Doubler claims, gives form to content.

Choreographers are guided in composing dances by the same principles used by other contemporary artists. The systematizing of a medium separates art from accident. The goal of composition, H'Doubler contends, is to create organic or "significant form," which is to fuse inner imagery with outward form. Her choice of words reflects Clive Bell's aesthetic standard[6] and John Martin's use of this phrase. Tools of the craft of composing dances help dancers structure movement patterns: unity, variety, contrast, balance, climax, sequence, transition, and repetition. For the layperson, H'Doubler summarizes these terms inadequately. A climax is a "rise to a turning point" which choreographers may choose to show in a variety of ways. "Stress in rhythm" helps vary movement sequences which contrast with previous rhythms to intensify what precedes or follows. "Strength of action" and "varying shades of feelings" modulate the quality and intensity of movements and add "richness and animation" to any dance composition (27). Unless one has dance experience, her explanations remain clouded by jargon.

H'Doubler attempts, unsuccessfully, to clarify the compositional process with a diagram in the shape of a spider web (fig. 1) unifying her

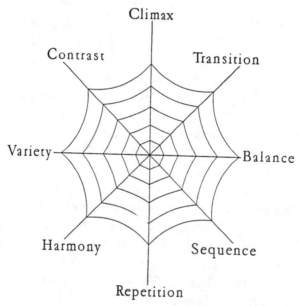

The composing of a dance may be compared to the spinning of a spider web. The pattern is woven from that which is within. In the process, structure is made possible by the medium's being fastened to supporting units (principles of composition). The pattern grows and takes its shape in accordance with inner necessity and the capacity, power, and excellence of execution.

FIGURE 1. H'Doubler's Diagram of Dance Composition

eight principles of composition and showing their equal importance and interconnectedness. The diagram can be misleading because not all the elements are equally important. She adds a schematic diagram of a loom (fig. 2) to demonstrate the interaction of the rhythmic, spatial, and form factors; this model suggests some practical movement studies for students learning how to compose. Her schematic representations indicate how to think about the parts of dance composition as a whole. When composing a dance, claims H'Doubler, dancers integrate the anatomical, physiological, and mental parts of themselves and develop a greater sense of individuality by using these tools in their own ways.

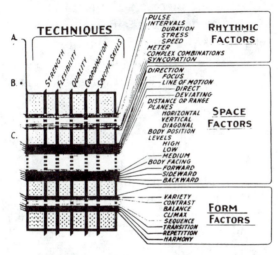

A. *Anatomical structure sets mechanical limits for motor response. The body is capable of flexion extension, abduction, adduction, rotation, circumduction, range and the activities of locomotion - walk - run - leap - hop - jump - simple combinations skip - gallop - slide. Their combinations offer an infinite variety of postures, gestures and actions.*

B. *Physiological determinants of movement are a consideration of physico-chemical processes and the neuro-muscular system. It is a behavior equipment possessing reflex paths and infinite possible activities that can be modified. It is by virtue of this structure that specific technical skills can be emancipated from diffuse responses. It is highly modifiable and must be educated by doing.*

C. *Mental equipment determines psychic behavior. (Is dependent upon B.) Here resides the awareness of all sensations as well as the capacity to think, feel, imagine, create, etc. It is the equipment for interpreting experience and developing a sense of values. This structure is the formative substance from which emerges personality. It is highly modifiable and educable and needs broad experience. It represents the personal human endowments that through knowledge and use are the only forces that lend warmth and significance to any act.*

A.-B.-C. Are the expression of racial and family heredities.

FIGURE 2. H'Doubler's Schematic Diagram of Dance Composition Factors

As an example, H'Doubler describes how a choreographer takes the feelings and idea of a lullaby and molds them into a dance using the principles of artistic composition. It would not be the best art form, she explains, to use just the realistic movements of holding and rocking. But, if the positions of holding and rocking were suggested, and the essential rhythms of the lullaby were used for the rhythms of the dance movement, these rhythms and positions would serve to suggest rather than produce the act itself (136).

Since H'Doubler does not discuss performance, she analyzes space as an element of composition but not as a feature of the setting. First, a dancer's sensitivity to space increases the emotive power of the movement; second, a dancer demonstrates an awareness of space by varying directions or levels; finally, a dancer's communicated feeling of "out-thereness" shows "the sense of relationship between self and space" (139). A dancer should move in, with, and through the space as though no boundaries exist.

H'Doubler's explanations of "space," "time," and "force" remain too general to adequately elucidate for non-dancers the unique physical qualities of a dance:

> Change of position implies that *direction* is taken and *distance* is covered. Movement has range. Also in covering distance, we consume time which further implies *rate* of movement or *execution*. And finally for movement to be accomplished at all, *energy* must be expended with some degree of force. (Italics added, 80)

Her explanation of space in this passage fails to specify how the dimensions of space—"change of position," "direction," "distance," and "range"—apply to the body parts, moving separately or together. "Covering distance," "rate of movement," and "execution," the carrying out of movement, happen in time, but H'Doubler does not indicate the kind of time—the music, the clock, the dancer's pulse. "Energy expended" simplifies "force" without suggesting the wide variations possible.

For H'Doubler, rhythm is the binding factor of all arts and a major source of dance themes. Other rhythmic arts such as poetry and music can also provide thematic stimuli for dances. Both music and dance express "abstract aspects of action" (154). Music is the constant partner of dance because it helps arouse the mood and supports the rhythmic basis of dance. Although in her earlier books, H'Doubler instructs dancers to base their dances on music, in 1940 she reverses her stance: agreeing with Selden, she recommends a musician compose a piece of music to accompany a specific dance. The dance, H'Doubler thinks, should be the primary focus for both dancer and audience; the music must not detract from it. Because the focus of her book is on the educational dimensions of dance, H'Doubler does not discuss lighting, costume, stage design, or props in conjunction with dance performance.

H'Doubler's discussion of the *process* remains unhelpfully abstract and over-general. Though she integrates technique, composition, settings, and other arts into the process of composing dances, her description leaves out improvisation as a way of finding new movements. Because she underscores the rational part of expression, her principles minimize the balance creative spontaneity provides to the intellectual part of art-making. Furthermore, she offers no criteria to determine if a dance communicates too much "physicality" and not enough "mind"; therefore, she offers no guidelines for evaluating dances. For readers from other fields, the ideas sound like guidelines for composing any art work, thus their uniqueness for dance remains unclear.

Observers

H'Doubler's viewpoint as an educator guides her analysis of *observers*. People watching dance receive its expressive communication through their eyes and ears and understand it through their kinesthetic sense: "Because [we] sympathize muscularly, we read ourselves into the line [of painting, architecture, dance performances] and observe how it would feel to move in their path" (138). H'Doubler regularly compares observing dance to the experience of appreciating other arts.

Beyond personal artistic expression, the other reason H'Doubler gives for the study of dance is to educate audiences to value dance as more than entertainment. Members of the audience need to understand dance as a vehicle of artistic expression and communication between the artist-dancer and the observer. Great art, she contends, depends on an audience's awareness of how art communicates its rich expressive qualities.

She aims to counteract the cultural bias of the early 1900s when dance was considered merely entertainment when seen in opera, musical comedy, vaudeville, and nightclub acts. Like Selden and Martin, H'Doubler, using a distorting dichotomy, insists that modern dance is art, not entertainment.

Since audience education is crucial to H'Doubler, she includes the functions of a critic in her theoretical exposition of dance. A critic writes informed responses to dance performances, educates audiences, clarifies "popular ideas of dance, and [is] a source of help to the dancer" (41). While she does not tie these critical functions to dance theory, she makes a plea for more critics able to write sensitive and impersonal evaluations of dance performances. Critics and members of the audience, she contends, base their evaluations on cultural values, contemporary experience, and personal preferences.

The Work

For H'Doubler, the dance as a work of art consists of two parts, the unseen inner dance and the outer observed dance. The work of art, a dance in its observed form, both expresses the choreographer's intentions and communicates these to observers.

> Dance is a rhythmic motor expression of feeling states, aes-
> thetically valued, whose movement symbols are consciously
> designed for the pleasure and satisfaction of re-experiencing,
> of communicating, or executing, and of creating form. (128)

H'Doubler's definition of a dance-work accepts the expression-communication theory of art and conceives of a dance as only a vehicle for expression, a means to achieve the end of communication.

Though the main purpose of a dance is to communicate the artist's aesthetic expression, H'Doubler does conceptualize a dance as an entity: "A dance, then, is a definite thing consisting of many parts that are interdependent." It is not ephemeral but is "a constructed form" (146), and as a physical entity, it is a mechanism for communication.

A dance expresses and communicates because it is "an image stimulus" (119). The two kinds of dances, representational and manifestive, stimulate different kinds of images. Representative dances often have dramatic content, with realistic imagery, themes, characters, and situations. (This is similar to Selden's "applied or illustrative" type.) Manifestive (Selden's "pure") dances are more abstract, originate from motor impulses, and use only the power of movement to arouse emotions. These, H'Doubler suggests, might be called dances of action and are presented in recital settings, whereas the representative dances are presented in theatrical settings. The source of both kinds of dance is the full range of human emotions; their quality ultimately depends on their emotional content.

Notating a dance, H'Doubler claims, is impossible because dance has so many complex elements. Though some systems have been tried, she finds them ineffective. Although the rhythmic structure can be notated, this record is only a tool of recall for the choreographer and a stimulus for other dancers; it does not provide a score. She suggests film as aid in maintaining a record of dances. Either a notation system or a film, for H'Doubler, serves primarily as an historical record, not as a means to theoretically understand a work of art-dance. The only lasting effect of a dance, H'Doubler argues, is in the visual memory of the onlooker and in the motor memory of the dancer.

The major fault with H'Doubler's view of *the work* is her focus on dance as a means to communicate and not an end in itself. Her analysis reflects the expression-communication theory of art without questioning its assumptions and implications. And because she deliberately avoids the common practice of highlighting specific dances of famous artists, she gives no examples to illustrate the many kinds of dances she describes in her categories of manifestive and representative dances. Therefore, H'Doubler's concept of a dance as only a vehicle for creative expression minimizes the physical bodily experience along with the sweat, fatigue, and exhilaration that go with dancing.

The Functions of the Process

Because the purpose of H'Doubler's book is to elaborate the educational benefits of dance, she includes the value system on which her objectives for dance in education are based. Dance provides individuals with "ample opportunity for spontaneous emotional release" (106) and stimulates each person's creative ability. She underscores the school's role in giving individuals an opportunity to express their uniqueness. This goal parallels the focus of psychological and educational reformers in the 1920s and 1930s who urged teachers to minimize the conforming aspects of schooling while maximizing opportunities for students to experience their originality in thinking and doing.

The study of dance creates an opportunity for the mind to train the body, and for the body to respond to the mind, both enhancing the kinesthetic sense, which bridges the mind-body duality. In dance classes, students channel their spontaneous physical and emotional release and thereby gain knowledge of their creative powers. Creative dance, as she called this type of experience, can give students understanding of all the arts. The study of dance must be broad enough to allow participants to dance according to their own capabilities; that is, the technical, rhythmic, kinesiological, and artistic range of the dance curriculum should be adapted to the varying levels of individuals and be flexible enough to train both professionals and amateurs.

H'Doubler's educational goals emerge from her knowledge of many styles of theater dance in history and contemporary society. She thinks the previous refined dance styles have almost obliterated the instinctive ability of people to express themselves in movement. Through movement education, teachers can revive the impulse to move expressively.

The teacher is the facilitator in the creative dance experience. For H'Doubler, the teacher demonstrates and explains the principles of good technique and innovative composition and guides the student dancer to utilize these principles and integrate the material. The development of students depends upon the teacher's ability to stimulate their artistic capabilities. A good teacher, H'Doubler claims, guides students to become their own teachers.

The study of the older dances of other cultures is pleasurable, and teachers should encourage today's dancers to compose dances reflecting their own culture. She believes "knowledge of folk forms is essential to a broad concept of dance" (32). H'Doubler's support for teaching these fixed forms demonstrates her breadth since her prime concern was with the creative activity of composing dances.

The Functions of the Work

H'Doubler's comprehensive view of dance incorporates dance in any social setting. The setting of dance determines its function: in ritual settings dance heightens group and individual feelings; in rural settings dance as a cultural expression preserves social and ethnic identity; in theatrical settings dance serves as a spectacle; in recreational settings dance uplifts dull spirits. Folk and ballroom dances are pleasurable activities which embody emotional experience common to all people. She explains how, in the past, professional court dance masters transformed folk dances into ballroom and theater dances; thus all forms of dance interchanged steps, styles, rhythms, costumes, and stories, thereby sharing their common expression.

The Material Studied

In the introduction of her book H'Doubler envisions dance as both an art, inviting the general study of a universal overview of dance, and a science, inviting the specific study of the workings of the physical body in motion. Kinesiology, the basis of dance science, offers valuable knowledge · about how the body works while dancing.

The Work Studied

The arts, H'Doubler repeatedly asserts, grow out of their past and reflect the cultural age in which they are produced. Her strongest unifying theme is this cultural continuity: "Art is ever the same, the effort to represent and interpret life . . . . Only its forms change" (107). The art of dance has always reflected the mental evolution of humanity, and dance works have always reflected individual and group roles which people play in their cultural milieu. Similar to Martin's notion of historical change in dance as only variations of style, the following statement summarizes H'Doubler's understanding of the interdependence of past and present, arts and culture, individual and group behavior:

> The differences between the dances of the past and those of the present are but differences in outer form: in period, location, temperament, education and taste, which together determine the cultural values of any age. Basically concerned

> with the primary issues of life, dance has been inseparably
> connected with the expression of the cultural development of
> any period and in turn has exerted its influence on the social
> patterns of the past. (45-46)

H'Doubler's concept goes beyond Martin's when she claims dance has influenced the development of culture. Instances of this influence are when
dancers' costumes became socially fashionable; and when men and women
experienced greater sexual freedom in the popular social dances of the
"jazz age": the Black Bottom, the Charleston, and the Jitterbug. The study
of dance history, H'Doubler insists, must therefore highlight changes of
cultural values and not just trace changes in techniques and choreographic
forms.

In her discussion of the *cultural context* for dance, as with other topics, H'Doubler offers few examples. Even in the chapter which surveys the
cultural history of dance she only summarizes historical periods, using the
developmental theory of history, and assumes her readers are familiar
with terms, historical events, and types of dances in the past. Without
many names and dates, her history remains on the level of fiction, while
her selective and derivative interpretation of dance history only clouds her
argument for the value of dance as a creative art.

The Theories of H'Doubler, Martin, and Selden

H'Doubler presents a comprehensive view of all forms and functions
of dance: "To appreciate the origin and nature of dance, to understand the
workings of its psychological-anatomical instrument and to be convinced
of its potentialities for emotional enrichment and self-direction is to know
the fundamental truth and enduring values of dance" (97). H'Doubler
conceives of the study of dance as interdisciplinary, as responsive to aesthetic needs, as accessible to everyone's experience, and as a universal
physical and aesthetic art expression.

Yet H'Doubler's discussion of dance neglects crucial professional
features of dance: professional dance training, performing at a high levels
of skill, choreographing for non-educational audiences, teaching to earn a
living, and teacher training. Her concentration on dance for enlightened
education overshadows the artistic drive dancers and choreographers
have to dance and choreograph dances.

Like Selden and Martin, H'Doubler's style is modeled on philosophic writing, which is abstract and general, relying on terms not clarified in the text though understood within the field. By overly conceptualizing the principles of dance, H'Doubler leaves out the physical and motional qualities unique to dance. Her reliance on the mind-and-body dichotomy misrepresents the holistic human being; dancing integrates a person's senses physically and experientially. Except in her discussion of the body, H'Doubler infrequently uses physical examples; this adds to the obscurity of her concepts.

Despite its limits, H'Doubler's theoretical writing about dance is comprehensive and even inspirational. Her book continues to be read by thousands of dance students in college and university dance departments. H'Doubler conceives of dance as an autonomous art form. The thrust of her book favors employing dance for expressive and communicative purposes of learning; encourages developing motor, creative, and aesthetic skills; and calls for understanding the social values of dance. However, H'Doubler, like Selden and Martin, overstates the expressive, communicative value of dance and does not give equal weight to the value of dance for its own sake.

Selden, Martin, and H'Doubler use the popular twentieth century expression-communication theory of art to explain the value of dance. Harold Osborne categorizes this theory as "instrumental" because it assumes that art functions to assist people in communicating with each other. Thus successful communication of emotion and experience is the criterion by which art is judged. The most recent version of this theory among our authors (H'Doubler's) emphasizes the creative function of art where the artist imaginatively contructs a new object which generates a new emotional experience for both artist and observer. Osborne believes artists and their supporters often write explanations of their activities in popular terms which more aptly explain art expression of the time immediately preceding their own, "without noticing that the assumptions implicit in their own practice are not conformable to these doctrines."[7] These three twentieth-century dance theorists, simply followed the traditional, innocent habit of trusting theoretical conceptualizations of aestheticians to explain the art activity in which modern dancers were involved.

The purpose that Selden, Martin, and H'Doubler give for writing their books of dance theory is to defend dance as an art; they all agree dance is worth experiencing for its own sake. The dance theorists do not recognize the contradiction inherent in accepting the then-current philosophic explanation of art. By using the popular expression-communication theory to explain that modern dance is art, the dance theorists devalue the physical, spatial phenomenon of dance as an entity, valuable in its own right, exclusive of its function as a stimulus for creative expression and communication. In claiming dance's primary significance is an expressive form of non-verbal communication, they understand dance as a means to an end and not an end in itself. They also overlook dance's importance as a cultural artifact because this concept depends on the recognition of dance as an entity.

If we place the ideas of Selden, Martin, and H'Doubler side by side, we find they agree with each other on most features of dance theory and share a broad conceptualization of the field of dance (Table 1). They include the artistic, scientific, historical, and educational features, and the social, entertainment, religious, and recreational functions and they frequently suggest how these dimensions of dance interrelate.

The negative consequence of using philosophic models to explain dance can be seen by examining what ideas are omitted or confounded by Selden, Martin, and H'Doubler. Though their discussions of dance works include the content, style, function, and setting of dances, they take the existence of actual dances for granted, focussing on the expressiveness of a dance rather than integrating its other parts into the description of the whole entity. The dance writers all know that dances *per se* exist and have intrinsic worth in their own right. Their analyses, however, minimize this dimension because of the philosophic model they apply to dance. And since few choreographers notate their dances, conceptualizing dances as entities is an unfamiliar approach.

In many instances, Selden, Martin, and H'Doubler do not offer operational definitions of the terms they use or else their usage is inconsistent. "Dancer" in their books of dance theory means the creating artist, the choreographer, the same way "painter" means the creating artist. The theorists assume their readers know the reason why modern dancers wanted to choreograph their own dances: modern dancers rebelled against the ballet tradition where only one or two choreographers monopolized this privilege. "Dancer," however, does not mean choreographer in folk dance, social dance, or ritual, and the theorists fail to make this distinction.

The theorists assume lay people have sufficient familiarity with general history and art to understand the frequent references to historical periods and art movements. Selden, Martin, and H'Doubler compound the problem of a reader's unfamiliarity with their references by not offering enough physical examples to explain their generalizations about art and dance. Their books are written by experts for other experts and assume their readers have dance experience. Without this experience non-dancers are likely to misunderstand their words. When Selden, Martin, and H'Doubler use metaphor and analogy in their explanations, they assume their readers have enough dance experience for their indirect expressions to be helpful. Not all readers are able to translate metaphorical indications into physical concepts about dance.

These critical comments are not meant to detract from the value of the theoretical writing just examined. Much of what Selden, Martin, and H'Doubler say is accurate, comprehensive, and clear, especially to readers familiar with dance. However, when readers with little or no dance experience depend on the writings of the dance theorists, the limitations of their work are magnified. Many of the aestheticians discussed in the following chapter depended on the books on dance theory of Selden, Martin, and H'Doubler as source material for their analyses of dance. The inadequacies of the dance theorists' writing contributed inadvertently to the aestheticians' confused and incomplete grasp of dance.

Other dance writers since Selden, Martin, and H'Doubler have borrowed philosophical models in writing dance theoretical books. Eleanor Metheny and Maxine Sheets-Johnstone accept Langer's theory of dance and explain why and how dance is expressive.[8] Sheets-Johnstone and Sondra Fraleigh use the existential phenomenology of Maurice Merleau-Ponty, Paul Ricoeur, and Hans Jonas to explain unique features of dance art: time, space, and force for Sheets-Johnstone, and the lived body for Fraleigh.[9] James Michael Friedman analyzes the ballet dancer in terms of theories of several aestheticians: Edward Bullough's concept of "psychical distance," Monroe Beardsley's notion of the "aesthetic object," and other

TABLE 1

SUMMARY COMPARISON OF SELDEN, MARTIN AND H'DOUBLER

	Selden	Martin	H'Doubler
Material			
Body	body and soul	mirror of all thought; pathfinder	outward aspect of personality
Kinesthetic sense	dancers depend on it; central to art-dance	communicates and receives all arts and dance	unifying function for body and senses
Movement	raw material for dance	source of dance movement	basis of dance movement
Dance Movement	motion, not emotion	dynamic, continuous flow of energy	natural, selected, and meaningful
Participants			
Dancer	means choreographer	means choreographer	means choreographer
Choreographer	makes group dances	dancer	dancer
Teacher	needs better training	———	teaches choreography
The Process			
Technique	frees the body to dance	to develop highly responsive instrument	aid to efficiency
Composition	Law of Materials: principles and feelings, harmony, balance, rhythm	form: time, space, dynamism, metakinesis	eight factors, to make form
Performance	performed in theater; space is material and setting	purpose of art, dance is in and with space	necessary for communication
Other arts	uses all, needs music	needs music, related to architecture and pantomime	like other rhythmic arts— poetry, music

	Selden	Martin	H'Doubler
Observers			
Audience	likes dramatic dances and variety	needs to learn that dance is easy to grasp	must be informed about art-dance
Critic	————	explains to audience, informs dancers	informs audience, helps dancers
The Work			
Aesthetic intention	universal-general: ideas, moods, feelings take physical shape	expresses and communicates universal emotional associations translated to action	expresses and communicates rhythmic personal feeling states in motion
Aesthetic result	motion: body to body	grasped kinesthetically new perception	kinesthetically experienced, body to body
Notation	mentioned, valuable, not widespread	should eliminate dance illiteracy	no adequate system, use of rhythmic notation
The Functions of the Process			
Education	to have public understand dance as art	for creative purposes not the same as professional	emotional release enhances creativity
Therapy	————	————	dance has therapeutic effects
The Functions of the Work			
Recreation Ritual Entertainment	fixed forms used communal function	functions described	settings and uses determine function
Materials Studied			
Kinesiology	———	valuable for theory and practice	important to study
Dance Studied			
Cultural Context	cultural context important, present connected to past	form and style depend on setting and purpose	dance and arts reflect their culture

ideas from Mikel Dufrenne and Guy Sircello.[10] Susan L. Foster applies
structuralist and post-structuralist theory (of Ferdinand de Saussure,
Claude Levi-Strauss, and Roman Jakobson) for her semiological analysis
of four contemporary choreographers.[11] Judith Lynne Hanna adopts theoretical constructs from several anthropologists, as well as Arthur
Koestler, D.E. Berlyne, and others who write aesthetic theory.[12] What
these dance writers say is generally carefully reasoned, interesting, stimulating, and informative. If, however, a criterion of good theory is its contribution to the clarification and development of dance practice, then much
of the work of these writers remains only an academic exercise of applied
theory.

NOTES

1 Margaret H'Doubler, *A Manual of Dancing* (Madison, Wis.: published by the author, 1921) and *The Dance and Its Place in Education* (New York: Harcourt Brace and Co., 1925).

2 Judith B. Alter, "Music and Rhythm in Dance: H'Doubler's Views in Retrospect," *Conference Proceedings, 1984* of the Society for Dance History Scholars (Riverside, Calif.: Unversity of California, Riverside, Dance Department, 1984).

3 Margaret H'Doubler, *Dance: A Creative Art Experience* (1940; rpt. Madison, Wis.: University of Wisconsin Press, 1959), xi. Further page references to this book will be cited parenthetically in the text in this chapter.

4 Judith Anne Gray, "To Want to Dance: A Biography of Margaret H'Doubler," Diss. University of Arizona 1978.

5 Yrjo Hirn, *The Origins of Art: A Psychological and Sociological Inquiry* (New York: The Macmillan Co., 1900), and John Dewey, *Art as Experience* (New York: Putnam's Capricorn Books, 1934, rpt. 1958).

6 Clive Bell, *Art* (London: Chatto and Windus, 1914).

7 Harold Osborne, *Aesthetics and Art Theory* (New York: E. P. Dutton, 1970), 12.

8 Eleanor Metheny, *Movement and Meaning* (New York: McGraw-Hill, 1968), and Maxine Sheets-Johnstone, *The Phenomenology of Dance* (Madison, Wis.: University of Wisconsin Press, 1966).

9 Sondra Fraleigh, *Dance and the Lived Body: A Descriptive Aesthetics* (Pittsburgh: University of Pittsburgh Press, 1988).

10 James Michael Friedman, *Dancer and Spectator: An Aesthetic Distance* (San Francisco: Ballet Monographs, 1976), and *Dancer and Other Aesthetic Objects* (San Francisco: Ballet Monographs, 1980).

11 Susan L. Foster, *Reading Dancing: Bodies and Subjects in Contemporary American Dance* (Berkeley and Los Angeles: University of California Press, 1986).

12 Judith Lynne Hanna, *To Dance Is Human* (Austin: University of Texas Press, 1979).

8

ELEVEN AESTHETICIANS ANALYZE DANCE

While Selden, Martin, and H'Doubler were carrying on the tradition of conceptualizing dance theory in terms borrowed from aestheticians, aesthetics changed. The methodological shift in philosophy set in motion by Ludwig Wittgenstein and the symbolic logicians which occurred in Europe and England in the 1930s and 1940s and in America in the 1950s greatly affected the kind of analysis aestheticians undertook. In their search for viable aesthetic inquiry, some aestheticians turned to the analysis of the language of visual art criticism. For the most part, those analyses excluded other art forms such as music and dance from consideration. Some aestheticians adapted a method similar to natural history: ordering, classifying, and comparing products and processes of the arts. Using that comparative method, the following aestheticians, writing between 1920 and 1966, analyze dance in their studies of the arts. (The initials after each name are used to identify the authors in this chapter.)

DeWitt Parker (DWP), *The Principles of Aesthetics*, 1920
Aram Torossian (AT), *A Guide to Aesthetics*, 1927
Theodore Meyer Greene (TMG), *The Arts and Art Criticism*, 1940
Louis W. Flaccus (LWF), *The Spirit and Substance of Art*, 1941
Friedrich Kainz (FK), *Aesthetics: The Science*, 1948
Thomas Munro (TM), *The Arts and Their Interrelations*, 1949
James K. Feibleman (JKF), *Aesthetics: A Study of the Fine Arts in Theory and Practice*, 1949
Morris Weitz (MW), *Philosophy of the Arts*, 1950
Paul Weiss (PW), *Nine Basic Arts*, 1961
Philip H. Phenix (PHP), *Realms of Meaning*, 1964
Etienne Gilson (EG), *Forms and Substances of the Arts*, 1966

Although these aestheticians primarily compare the features, properties, and functions of the arts they analyze, several also offer a summary definition of each art. As an introduction to the variety of approaches found in their studies, here are definitions of dance by seven of the aestheticians.

Torossian: "The dance is the art of expressing a bit of experience in terms of human values through movements of one or more human forms."[1]

Flaccus: "Dance is a fusion of space and time impressions . . . the visualizing and imaginative ordering of impulses and emotions in close relation to the motor life of the body. It is a constantly renewed interchange of freedom and order . . . of energy taking rhythmic form and form turned back to energy."[2]

Munro: "Dance is an art of rhythmic bodily movement, presenting to the observer an ordered sequence of moving visual patterns of line, solid shape, and color. The postures and gestures of which these are made suggest kinesthetic experience of tensions, relaxation, etc. and emotional moods and attitudes associated with them. Dances are performed by one person or by two or more in mutual coordination."[3]

Weiss: "The dance is a world in which the individual becomes one with the dance, pouring energy into a single whole or energy which thereby iconizes, with hardly any mediation, the nature of an existential becoming."[4]

Parker: "Dance consists . . . in the free and rhythmical expression of impulses to movement."[5]

Feibleman: "Dance is an art in which the human body exclusively is employed in order to actualize values beyond the human which were not hitherto actualized, or to enrich such values having but a tenuous hold on existence."[6]

Gilson: "The dance is the art which orders the natural bodily movements by imparting to them a form which is pleasing in itself, independently of any other end."[7]

The definitions emphasize the motivations for making dances and generally lack words conveying the physicality of dance activity. They simplify dance to such an extent that if we did not know what dancing was, it might be impossible to use any of them to identify a dance. Substitute jogging, acting, playing, or praying for "dance" in these definitions and many of them would continue to make sense. In their definitions, Flaccus, Weiss, Parker, and Gilson use the collective noun "dance" referring to the field, where "a dance," singular, might make their definitions more precise and useful in identifying a dance.

Weiss crowds his definition with undefined philosophical jargon, such as "world," "iconizes," and "the nature of existential becoming." He severely obscures the dynamic and time factors while limiting the variety of meanings dances have by identifying the basic one as "becoming." Torossian's explanation of the meaning of dance as "human values" is similarly vague. He, like Feibleman, confounds the means with the end: movement is the point of dance whether or not it conveys any "idea" or "value." Flaccus's definition uses mechanical metaphors and omits human beings while Torossian abstracts the dancers into "forms." Such abstract words are appropriate in the domain of philosophy, but fail to transfer to dance theory because they omit too much essential information. These attempts to define dance are good examples of why contemporary philosophers decided to stop asking unanswerable questions, such as "What is dance?"

Constructing simple definitions is not the primary focus of these eleven aestheticians in their analysis of the arts. They intend to examine each art objectively to compare them. They identify their physical, technical features, and their compositional, presentational, and aesthetic dimensions. Though their discussions of dance vary in mode and detail, the aestheticians consider many of the same topics.

Throughout this chapter are summary charts of the aestheticians' ideas about the features and dimensions of dance organized into the main divisions of my Framework of Topics Intrinsic to Dance Theory. In the charts I compile the philosophers' words and categories to illustrate the similarities and differences among their analyses of dance. Most of the eleven aestheticians, Table 1 shows, wrote at least one entire chapter about dance, ranging in length from ten to twenty pages. The table illustrates how dance was considered by these aestheticians as equal to the

TABLE I
LENGTH OF DISCUSSION AND DANCE SOURCE

Author	Length of Discussion	Dance Sources
Parker 1920	brief mention	———
Torossian 1927	1 chapter	Elizabeth Selden Isadora Duncan
Greene 1940	5 brief sections 1 six-page section	Elizabeth Selden Cecil Sharp and Adolf Oppe John Martin Martha Hill Havelock Ellis Mary Wigman
Flaccus 1941	2 chapters	Havelock Ellis Jane Harrison John Martin Troy and Margaret Kinney
Kainz 1948	several brief mentions	Paul Souriau Rudolf Laban
Munro 1949	26 mentions 1 six-page section	many and varied
Feibleman 1949	1 chapter	no bibliography cited
Weitz 1950	1 brief section	Margaret H'Doubler Elizabeth Selden John Martin
Weiss 1961	1 chapter	John Martin Doris Humphrey Merle Mariscano Ted Shawn Jean Noverre Merce Cunningham

Phenix 1964	1 chapter	John Martin Margaret H'Doubler Margaret Lloyd Elizabeth Hayes Frederick Rogers Walter Sorell
Gilson 1966	1 chapter	no bibliography cited

other arts during the very time when members of the dance community thought dance was neglected in aesthetic literature.

This table also shows the dance sources the eleven aestheticians used as reference. These include books written by theorists Selden, Martin, H'Doubler, and Laban; historians Margaret and Troy Kinney, Jane Harrison, and Cecil Sharp; critics Margaret Lloyd and Walter Sorell; educators Elizabeth Hayes and Frederick Rogers; and man of letters Havelock Ellis. Only three aestheticians used the writings of choreographers: Torossian read Isadora Duncan, Greene refers to Mary Wigman, and Weiss cites Jean Georges Noverre, Doris Humphrey, Merle Mariscano, Ted Shawn, and Merce Cunningham.

The Material

The physical medium of dance (see Table 2), the astheticians agree, is the human body, with its coordinated moving parts, its intrinsic physical qualities and abilities, and its full range of movement between motion and rest. Gilson and Munro point out how the bodies of dancers vary in power, strength, range of motion, speed, suppleness, endurance, as well as natural beauty. Munro thinks psychological and personality factors affect how a dancer performs. Only Gilson argues that dancers have a special intelligence, where the mind and body are a "'substantial union.' The born dancer thinks with his body the way he dances with his mind. . . . No other art [uses] the human being in the organic unity of all his constitutive material and spiritual elements."[8]

TABLE 2
THE MATERIALS

Author	Sense	Kind	Physical Media	Aesthetic Media
Parker	motor visual	rhythmic movement	dancer's body in motion	indirect and ideal
Torossian	visual tactile	movement temporal	dancer's body movement and rest	glorified gesture
Greene	kinesthetic visual	rhythmic movement	bodily movement in space and time	emotions, conative attitudes symbolic
Flaccus	visual kinesthetic	living body in time and space	patterned bodily movement	rhythm pose gesture costume setting
Kainz	motor kinesthetic	time and space	human form movement ordered	emotional symbolic gestural
Munro	auditory visual kinesthetic	movement for dancer, visual and audial for audience	physical body power of rhythmic movement	color line texture solid shape in time
Feibleman	total person	plastic movement auditory into future	human body infinite variety of movement	body objectified
Weitz	———	human body	body's intrinsic qualities dynamic	space time weight

Weiss	visual	space	body and	emotion
	motor	time	gravity	dynamic
	emotional	becoming	rhythm	movement
			rest	space
Phenix	motor	time	human body	abstract
		weight		movement
Gilson	total person	time and	body and	————
		space	intelligence	

Most of the aestheticians agree dance communicates by the kinesthetic sense, though some choose "tactile" or "motor" to identify the specific physicality of dance. The word "communicates" in their explanations of dance assumes two-way interaction, but only Feibleman and Munro clearly identify the kinesthetic sense as central for the dancer and the audience. Even they do not explain how the kinesthetic sense functions in both audience and dancers. Half the authors (DWP, AT, TMG, LWF, TM, PW) also categorize dance as "visual"; Munro adds "auditory." Only Feibleman and Gilson realize that dance communicates to and by means of the total person.

When describing what kind of art dance is, five aestheticians (DWP, AT, TMG, TM, JKF) agree dance is an art of movement, while five (LWF, FK, PW, PHP, EG) describe it as the art of space and time. Most do not explain the meaning of these terms, though for Feibleman and Weiss, time in dance is "into the future" and "becoming" to accent the ongoing, continuous fleetingness of performing it.

Movement—idealized, objectified, abstracted, and dynamic—the aestheticians agree, is the aesthetic medium of dance, though most realize dance movement does not have specific literal connotations. Greene, Weiss, and Kainz claim movement is emotionally expressed. Although the writers distinguish among dance movement, everyday gesture, and pantomime, none explain how any human movement becomes source material for dance movement.

The greatest lack of clarity the aestheticians exhibit in their understanding of the *Material* of dance derives from their point of view. Some write from only the dancer's point of view, some from only the audience's point of view; only Munro writes from both. This failure can be traced to their sources; the point of view from which the dance theorists write is not always clear, as we have seen. Consulting the books of those theorists about dance, the aestheticians fail to understand the value of such perceptual distinctions.

The Process

The eight aestheticians who discuss technique (see Table 3) identify its function, not its essence. The following description exemplifies this sort of explanation: Technical skill is required for adroit physical coordination, modulated breathing, and conscious emotional control. Technical facility is also necessary to facilitate change in direction, weight displacement, and forward progress. The aestheticians write extremely general descriptions: were their ideas not within an essay on dance, their explanations of dance technique would easily apply to other activities, such as athletics, public speaking, or theater.

Torossian and Greene explain how a dancer must skillfully coordinate expressive movements performed in formal patterns. Phenix differentiates between ballet technique, a codified set of steps and floor patterns to be mastered, and modern dance technique developed by individuals to be universally expressive. He details how modern dance technique trains dancers for strength, control, plasticity, responsiveness, and mastery of emotional objectification. Weiss recognizes other functions of technique: it enables dancers to defy or respond to gravity, to channel energy in a distinctive way, and to express movement themes with ease and grace.

Only Gilson cites the names of ballet steps in his description of dance technique. These steps function, he argues, as a cohesive means of structuring ballet movement patterns. Comparing dance to language, he writes of ballet, "The grammar of this speech is represented by the five elementary positions of the feet." The dancer, he explains, "will probably have to master this gymnastic training and learn this syntax of motion."9 National styles of folk dance, he claims, also have specific grammars of motion. Though he never reveals how dance positions, steps, and training fit together, Gilson's analysis of the body, its training, and technique are more thorough than any of the other philosophers writing comparative analyses.

TABLE 3
THE PROCESS

Author	Technique	Composition
Parker	———	———
Torossian	skill formal patterns coordination	theme repetition emotional tension
Greene	mastery of steps formal patterns emotional expression correct execution	formal or free form has beginning, middle and end with rhythm and music unitary idea
Flaccus	schematized dress and pose—Ballet	selected movement organized for expression
Kainz	———	———

Munro	posture and gesture
	    coordinated
		called choreography
		pictorial or sculptural patterns
		    with music

Feibleman	rhythm and grace the means of performance	theme and time variations poses, formal patterns from improvisation
Weitz	———	———
Weiss	ease and grace	structured themes climax of expression

Phenix	Ballet: conventions
	Modern: strength,
	    control, emotions
	    mastered
		movement idea
		theme and variations
		climax, emotional
		    objectification

Gilson	grammar of motion gymnastic freedom with virtuosity	choreographer improvises creative imagination plastic forms unfolding

The aestheticians approach dance composition in several ways. For Flaccus and Gilson, the term "composition" refers to the process of making a dance, while for others it refers to the features of a dance itself (AT, TMG, TM, JKF, PW, PHP). Though the theorists agree modern dance has no widely established method for composing dances, several realize modern dances have movement themes which are varied, repeated, and ordered in visual and abstract patterns. Greene, who quotes much information from Martin's *America Dancing*, gives examples of the choreographic methods of four modern dance pioneers. He explains how they individually develop their physical or ideational themes into movement patterns with music, costume, and setting.

The philosophers who examine composition are confused about its basis. They think a codified technical vocabulary of movement, as in ballet, dictates a prescribed method of choreography. In contrast, they assume choreographers who use modern dance technique and compose dances in free form do not adhere to any method of structuring dances. The thinkers fail to understand that neither ballet nor modern dance have compositional methods which compare to the rules of harmony in music. Yet freedom in dance composition does not automatically mean no guidelines exist. Both ballet and modern dance have compositional methods; neither dance style is rigid or formless. This confusion may be due to the failure of the dance theorists to make this point clear in their books.

In discussions of the formal structure of dance, the aestheticians identify the features of a dance's composition with terms such as "time" and "space" which are used to study all the arts; indeed, these terms have been used in aesthetics for several centuries. Dances, assert our authors, are made up of ordered or organized patterns of abstract movement in space. Feibleman and Phenix point to theme and variation, the device used in structuring musical composition, as a way of ordering movement sequences. Like music, eight of the thinkers explain, dance is structured in time and uses rhythmic patterns.

Torossian and Phenix identify projected emotions as part of the composed dance, but only Phenix considers the element of force ("control") as an integral part of dance's structure. Force, which modulates weight and time by energy control, is a difficult part of dance to put into words. The most dynamic and electrifying component of a dance's communicating power, force, like tone color in music, individualizes a composition and a performance. That only one aesthetician discusses force shows a regrettable inadequacy in the dance sources and a damaging omission on the part of the philosophers.

Dance, all the writers agree, is performed with music (see Table 4, next page). A few mention attempts by the modern dance choreographer Doris Humphrey and ballet choreographer Jerome Robbins to compose dances with no accompaniment. Whenever possible, some explain, music should be composed to fit the needs of the dance rather than the dance being composed to fit the music. Costume, lighting, settings, and stage decoration, they agree, are often part of a dance performance, though only Flaccus, Greene, Feibleman, and Weitz explain how early modern dance choreographers deliberately chose to minimize the stage effects to emphasize the dances.

To the aestheticians, manner of treatment means dances are done in solo, duet, or group performances. This category stems from their comparison of dancers with musicians, who often play in large groups, or with painters and sculptors who work alone. Feibleman and Munro also identify dance as a social art, incomplete until performed for an audience.

The location of art-dance, eight aestheticians agree, is on a theater stage, in space. Munro calls it deep space. Phenix identifies space around the body as intrinsic to dance's setting. Munro and Phenix touch on the unique part space plays in contemporary dance, but their audience point of view prevents them from also identifying space as a primary physical-aesthetic material for dance. Here, Weiss construes space from the outside: "If a dancer is alone, he dances not only where his body is but in the entire dancing space."[10] If a dancer had written this it might read "with the entire dance space" or even "shaping the entire dance space" to show how dancers sculpt space as well as their bodies when they dance. Although Flaccus, Munro, and Feibleman identify ballrooms, sacred spaces, and temples as settings for social and ritual dance, their emphasis on art-dance causes them to neglect the similarities among all forms of dance.

Dance-Based Dance Theory

TABLE 4
THE PROCESS, CONTINUED:

Author	Formal Structure	Supports	Manner of Treatment	Location
Parker	———	music costume	———	theater

Torossian	like music
	rhythm
	theme and
	    variation
	abstract pattern
		music
		costume
		setting
		decoration
			one or more
			forms an organic
			    unit
			recreated
				stage

Greene	no prescribed
	    beginning,
	    middle, end,
	    music—formal
	    or free
		music
		costume
		setting
		    or none
			solo
			duet
			choral
			mimetic or not
				———

Flaccus	mobile visual rhythm emotional dramatic	sets lights costume music always	solo group tribal circle	space hall
Kainz	angles, forms measure, order, repetition	———	———	———
Munro	deep space ordered sequences visual pattern time	music costume sets lights	solo couple group	theater ballroom religious ground

Feibleman	uses bodies,
	form and
	    materials
		costumes
		scenery
			social art
			one or more
			    people
			audience
				theater
				ritual and
				    social spaces

Weitz	carried out in real motion	music weight decor narrative poetic recitation	solo group	————
Weiss	time, space form, design rhythm, emotion	music audience gravity theatrical elements	————	unique space stage with audience
Phenix	steps, space time, weight inner logic costume architecture	music sets lights	————	stage space with body in space
Gilson	space time	music always sets, lights decor	solo duet group	space

The Work

The dance in performance (see Table 5) is the work of art; thus the process is also the product. The dance itself, however, is separate from the dancer and exists in the same way a poem or song exists whether or not it is being performed. By pointing out how the same dance is recreated anew for each performance, the aestheticians implicitly acknowledge the dance-work exists. The idea of dance as an entity contrasts with the spontaneous appearance of dancing in performance. The dance theorists fail to explain how a dance is carefully rehearsed to follow the exact specifications of the choreographer; therefore no philosopher includes this part of the production process.

The expression of human feelings and psychic impulses, the aestheticians conclude, is the primary subject matter of dance. Abstract patterns and visual forms, according to Greene, Flaccus, and Feibleman, are also subject matter because movements can be symbolic as well as purely decorative. Some of the aestheticians think dance and music evoke feelings in audiences in similar ways. Munro, Feibleman, and Weiss realize dance can convey a story. Parker believes men only enjoy dance when

TABLE 5
THE WORK

Author	Subject Matter	Function
Parker	movement real and felt emotions	for its own sake for men to fall in love
Torossian	decorative expression of feelings human impulses	non-purposive descriptive
Greene	directly expressive pure, symbolic	new truths
Flaccus	feelings, impulses visual form symbolic or not	dancing, work, or pastime
Kainz	psychic qualities	— —
Munro	human expressions moods, characters stories	theatrical decorative
Feibleman	patterns: as many as music symbolic of emotion any human occasion	expression of emotion
Weitz	expressiveness gesture dynamic body	abstract, common ideas expression
Weiss	story experience feelings	abstract, myth theatrical rhythmic
Phenix	human emotions	expression mind-body unity play
Gilson	— — —	motion

they feel "amorous feelings" for the dancers; he seems unconcerned about the responses of the women in the audience.

In addition to the categories of subject matter and function of the *work* the aestheticians grapple with dance's expressiveness and notation (Table 6). To explain how dance is expressive, the eleven aestheticians compare it to language. How the arts compare with language is a recurrent twentieth-century philosophic concern. The aestheticians characterize dance's expressive language in three ways: as "glorified gesture"[11] or a universal language of everday gesture, as mystic, and as symbolic. It is symbolic, Phenix asserts, of the "life of persons at the well-springs of organic being."[12] Gilson carries this idea further when he claims "the speech in motion, which is what a dance is, bears the mask of a definite style which is that of this speech itself."[13] Gilson's "speech in motion" could be interpreted as dance movements conveying specific meanings similar to words, yet dance movements do not convey translatable meanings in the way words do, nor do dance movements belong in prescribed logical sequences. None of the aestheticians makes these distinctions clear or identifies the word "language" as a metaphor for an expressive symbol system.

The philosophers' explanations of the expressive features of dance reveal the way dances convey meaning. These explanations fall into two groups. One explanation shows dance as abstract, signifying itself the way an abstract painting displays its own uniquely presented meaning. The other explanation sees the set of structures of a dance as symbolic. Weiss asserts:

> Precisely because it has no story to tell, the dance can easily be misconstrued as presenting nothing but a set of structures. There is more to dance than this. It has meaning imbedded in it. . . . Dance makes evident the nature of myth. This is a cultural idea referring to and making relevant an objective meaningful ideal. . . . Dance tries to do nothing more than convey the unitary meaning of a beginning, middle and end.[14]

This paragraph exemplifies an extreme form of abstract analysis characteristic of philosophy. Dances do, at times, convey stories; Weiss has oversimplified for the sake of his argument. Dances are more than the

TABLE 6
THE WORK, CONTINUED

Author	Expressiveness	Notation
Parker	rhythmic form amorous subject interpreted	————
Torossian	abstract patterns pure feelings recreated, interpreted	————
Greene	direct dramatic expression recreated, interpreted	terminology, script necessary to develop for study memory limited
Flaccus	self activity experienced directly rhythmic play	film shows patterns mentions lack
Kainz	feeling for form psychic content moving living bodies	————
Munro	general aesthetic recreated	not major because no written tradition film can help
Feibleman	re-interprets aesthetic impulses	necessary to preserve form, analyze past, study performances film can help
Weitz	pure expression symbolic	————
Weiss	energy defy gravity interpreted	————
Phenix	life re-interpreted new worlds idealized inward purposes moods and kinds of feeling objectified	needed for history, past and present retrieval, diffusion

Gilson	speech in motion	ballet terms are necessary to
	expression is not	maintain tradition
	imitiation	benefits similiar to a musical score
		necessary

celebration of a beginning, middle, and end, though they have this structure. Weiss does not clarify what he means by "the nature of myth,"
though his explanation refers to the Aristotelian notion of "form" in art.
The "unitary meaning" of dance is the way Weiss identifies the form of a
dance as an entirety, seen and remembered from its beginning to its end.
His words do not give a clear picture of this idea.

The philosophers present the functions of dance-art in two ways: as
purely decorative, abstract, for its own sake and for personal pleasure;
and as the expression of human or universal emotions, motion, or rhythmic play. Echoing Plato, Flaccus sees dance as valuable for the physical
training of the body. For the most part, the explanations of the functions
of dance by the philosophers extend their analyses of its meaning and its
expressive language.

Six aestheticians (TG, LF, TM, JF, PP, EG), offer discerning reasons
why dances need to be notated. With the notation of dances, they claim,
the field of dance would have a recorded past and thus a way of retrieving
and studying its history. Photographic records, all agree, are insufficient
for providing a real sense of a dance although motion pictures would offer
a partial record. Notation, they argue, would stabilize each dance-work
and allow it to be transmitted via a universal symbolic language. This
symbol system would be a tool for teaching dances of the present and from
the past. If not recorded, Gilson and Feibleman argue, a dance exists only
in the limited memories of dancers and ceases to exist after its performance or when the dancer dies. If choreographers were to use a notation
system when composing, teaching, and directing their dances, these aestheticians believe, they would have the range, freedom, and resources
available to musicians, composers, actors, and directors. Their conclusions
about the value of dance notation amplify the suggestions of the dance
theorists about its importance.

Notation, the aestheticians assert, offers other benefits. Development and analysis of the art form are possible with the use of a score because a dance can be exactly identified and repeated from performance to performance. A few of the aestheticians are aware of Laban's notation system, developed in 1927, and they feel it could function on the many levels just described. None of the aestheticians identifies the limits of the current notation systems or realizes how, for the past 3,000 years, many people in dance have attempted to formulate and use some type of dance notation.

The Work Studied

Ten philosophers discuss forms of dance other than art-dance, most commonly ballroom and folk (see Table 7), though they categorize the functions of these non-art types of dance differently: religious and social; entertainment and ritual; gymnastic, decorative, mimetic, pantomimic, and aesthetic; functional and emotional. Though the philosophers explain how art-dance differs from other types, few realize how these others serve the art as source material for movement, structure, music, and story.

Seven aestheticians (AT, TMG, TM, LWF, MW, PHP, EG) refer to the origin of dance as the oldest universal art activity and a basic part of life, religion, and play. Dance theorists thought claiming dance to be the universal initial art would contribute to raising its status from a popular to a fine art. Perhaps the philosophers echo this claim to justify their considering dance among the fine arts. Munro identifies two central obstacles early twentieth-century dance artists confronted when trying to achieve art status for dance: the lingering social stigma against the "physical arts" and the limits of dance's oral history.

Implications

The philosophers undertake a descriptive analysis of the arts; thus their purpose limits the depth of their analyses. Despite this limitation, their comparative stance sheds light on many issues crucial to dance theory. The status of dance as an art is definitive for these eleven aestheticians. This should reassure members of the dance community who feel dance is not recognized by philosophers as an art. Equally significant, the

TABLE 7

THE WORK STUDIED

Author	Other Types	Origin
Parker	theater communal religious	————
Torossian	ballet, free form, ballroom, folk pre-classic, Greek choral	very old
Greene	religious, social, ballet, free form great variety influence stage forms	one of oldest most universal

Flaccus	gymnastic, pantomimic
	  decorative, mimetic
	  aesthetic;
	interpretive or classical
		basic to life
		religion and play

Kainz	modern, ballet	————
Munro	entertainment ritual, folk, ballet, modern—expressive physical education, recreation	————

Feibleman	folk, ritual, court
	  art (modern)
		universal
		  part of human activity

Weitz	————	————
Weiss	ballet, modern, social, ritual	oldest art
Phenix	ethnic—crystallized ballet—formalized modern—expressive	earliest most elemental
Gilson	religious, communal, erotic, artistic	first discovered art

philosophers depended on dance sources for their understanding of the art. This may explain why, until the 1960s, the majority of philosophers focussed primarily on modern dance and excluded ballet: such an emphasis also characterizes the dance theory books. Though the emphasis is changing, most contemporary dance writing still treats ballet and modern dance separately. The idea of mind-body separation, still pervasive in contemporary popular thinking, is absent in the discussions of dance covered above. Gilson uses the mind-body dichotomy ironically to discuss the unity of a person's faculties in his concept of the dancer's "thinking body and dancing mind."

A crucial observation emerges from this study of the views of the eleven authors: notation can serve the theoretical and practical development of dance. The issue of notation for dance, identified and described by these writers, illustrates how thinkers outside the field recognized a serious impediment to the formulation of dance theory. Without widespread use of notation systems, the field of dance will depend on oral history, and dance history books will feature the dancers rather than the dances.

The comparative method of analysis severely limits comprehension of the complex holistic physical experience of dance. This method sacrifices specificity for generality. An instance of this generality is when the aestheticians apply terms such as "time," "space," "social," "expression," and "language" to all the arts. They overlook how practitioners in each art understand these terms within their own contexts where meanings vary. Even when the philosophers define some of their terms, the variations crucial to the uniqueness of each art are glossed over. None of these writers includes a glossary of terms.

Another limitation of this method of analysis is the level of abstraction necessitated by the brief expositions of each art. The consequences of these abstract descriptions are evident in the seven definitions of dance and in the explanations of technique discussed above. Though abstraction and generalization are a requisite part of the discipline of philosophy, these characteristics of writing and analysis do not aptly transfer to writing a theoretical explication of dance nor are they meant to transfer.

Sometimes the philosophers conflate the points of view from which they describe dance. Though they most often assume the audience point of view, at times they interweave the perspective of the creator or performer into their analyses. For example, in discussing the sense by which dance is experienced, several aestheticians inadvertently combine the viewpoint of audience members who see, hear, and kinesthetically identify with the dance and the viewpoint of the dancer who experiences dancing the dance with all the senses.

The confusion exhibited in the aestheticians' writings stems partly from their dance sources. The dance theorists confound the dancer and the dance. This confusion in turn contributes to the conflation of viewpoints in several of the topics discussed by the aestheticians. The separation of viewpoints in writing dance theory, I contend, is as important as maintaining connections between other aspects of dance in a theoretical framework. Though the aestheticians use theoretical sources written by dance experts, their conclusions are inconsistent with each other and with those of the dance experts. A glance at the summary charts shows this inconsistency.

The Framework of Topics Intrinsic to Dance Theory facilitates identifying one more limitation of this type of philosophic analysis, its incompleteness. These aestheticians omit important features such as improvisation and production; fail to differentiate among features of composition, the aesthetic intention, and the aesthetic result of the work; and overlook such dimensions as the functions of the process and the process studied. Though stimulating and informative, their understanding of dance is limited by both their method of analysis and their dance sources.

Recently David Best and Francis Sparshott have written aesthetic theories about dance using neither the comparative method of analyis nor the expression-communication theory as a base.[15] Though both these philosophers are much more sensitive to the scholarly considerations of dance than many of the aestheticians analyzed thus far, they write about dance as philosophers and are guided by the research paradigm of their field: the purpose of writing a theory is to correct the theories previously written by other philosophers. Their work is thus idea-based, not dance-based, and intellectually powerful but not physically inclusive.

NOTES

1 Aram Torossian, *A Guide to Aesthetics* (Palo Alto, Calif.: Stanford University Press, 1927), 182.

2 Louis W. Flaccus, *The Spirit and Substance of Art* (New York: F.S. Crofts, 1941), 76-79.

3 Thomas Munro, *The Arts and Their Interrelations* (New York: The Liberal Arts Press, 1949), 496.

4 Paul Weiss, *Nine Basic Arts* (Carbondale, Ill.: Southern Illinois University Press, 1961), 104.

5 DeWitt Parker, *The Principles of Aesthetics* (Boston: Silver, Burdett, 1920), 148.

6 James K. Feibleman, *Aesthetics: A Study of the Fine Arts in Theory and Practice* (New York: Duell, Sloan, and Pearce, 1949), 311.

7 Etienne Gilson, *Forms and Substance of the Arts* (New York: Scribner's Sons, 1966), 186.

8 Gilson, 191.

9 Gilson, 194-195.

10 Weiss, 210.

11 Torossian, 186.

12 Philip H. Phenix, *Realms of Meaning* (New York: McGraw-Hill, 1964), 167.

13 Gilson, 194.

14 Weiss, 212-213.

15 David Best, *Expression in Movement and the Arts* (London: Lepus Books, 1974), *Philosophy and Human Movement* (London: George Allen and Unwin, 1978), and Francis Sparshott, *Off the Ground: First Steps to a Philosophical Consideration of Dance* (Princeton: Princeton University Press, 1988).

9

DANCE IN THE AESTHETIC THEORY OF
NELSON GOODMAN

For centuries, aestheticians have grappled with how the arts are meaningful. Although the aestheticians who compared the properties and functions of the arts sidestepped this issue, other twentieth-century philosophers have been preoccupied with the meaning of meaning. Words, pictures, gestures, and so on can have several levels of meaning: literal, expressive, referential, and symbolic. The symbolic meaning of art gained prominence among the aestheticians in this century as one solution to the problem of art's value, function, and meaning; Langer and several others agree that, like language, the arts are symbolically expressive, but they disagree about how. Nelson Goodman places language alongside other symbol systems in his book *Languages of Art* and presents a method for analyzing the symptoms of art rather than generating closed definitions of it. The publication of the first edition of his book in 1968 revived the field of aesthetics because he provides analytical methodology for thinking about the arts and generates answerable questions, such as "When is art?" Goodman's expertise in symbolic logic enhances his ability to find new resolutions for questions aestheticians have debated for centuries. He demonstrates how several useless and misleading dichotomies found in older aesthetic theories obstruct thinking: mind-body, cognitive-emotive, subjective-objective, real-abstract, theory-practice, and art-science.

In the introduction to *Languages of Art*, Goodman translates his title to "Symbol Systems of Art." Carefully "sorting . . . features, elements and processes," he traces two themes while analyzing how different symbol systems, including dance, communicate.[1] First, by clarifying the relations among the meanings of denotation, representation, and expression in art and other symbol systems, he explains not only how art communicates but why it does so. Second, he identifies the distinguishing features of notations and terms associated with them from languages and nonlanguages.

He then operationally ties the two themes together to characterize aesthetic "symptoms" of all arts in relation to aesthetic experience.

Goodman has produced dance works and helped start the Harvard Summer School of Dance; this direct experience in dance is unusual for an aesthetician. The question ("Can dance be notated?") which stimulated his writing *Languages of Art* grew out of his dance experience. He consulted the work on notation and the writings by Laban for information about dance. Goodman's arguments about the role of notation, the way arts communicate their "meaning," and the symptoms or features of the arts have had major impact on both philosophy and dance.

Goodman's analyses shed light on many of the issues examined by Collingwood, Langer, and the comparative aestheticians. Unlike the others, Goodman writes about art from a multiple viewpoint which includes the creator, the performer, and the observers. But because of the depth of his dance knowledge, his arguments go beyond philosophy to the heart of formulating a comprehensive theory for dance.

The Material

What Goodman asserts about the body participating in all arts is fundamental to dance. He confronts the dichotomy of the arts as either rational or emotional. For him, aesthetic experience and invention combine cognitive, dynamic, and sensory activity; cognitive activity includes sensory and emotive experience. Art activity, the invention and interpretation of symbols, is grasped by our minds and our bones and nerves and it requires the participation of our bodies' total sensitivity and responsiveness. For the outworn mind-body dichotomy, Goodman substitutes the total unit of a person's active capabilities. The body participates in all communication as it does in dance. And since for Goodman the body is the physical manifestation of a total human being, the entire person participates actively in the processes of inventing and presenting dance.

Goodman examines how the kinesthetic sense, by means of the muscles, participates with the other senses in human expression and experience. When discussing modes of reference and how people analyze, organize, and register works of art, Goodman contends that perception is active, not passive. Psychologists and linguists, he points out, stress the value of gestural and sensory-motor activity in the cognitive development of children. As an example of the benefits of physical learning, he cites the teaching methods of Emile Jaques-Dalcroze, the Swiss music teacher who taught musicians and dancers during the early twentieth century. Jaques-Dalcroze required music students to use their entire bodies to learn music and rhythm. Sensory response, for Goodman, is part of the cognitive process in which the senses function cooperatively and interactively in processing information including that from the arts.

Goodman knows how everyday movement plays a part in dance. He cites the opinions about the universality of gestures of choreographer Doris Humphrey and anthropologist Ray Birdwhistell: Many physical ways exist to express feelings, though none are universal; gestures emerge from, and are only significant in the context of, a culture. Goodman identifies the role which non-verbal forms of communication play in dance movement when he shows how dances utilize denotative gestures from daily life, such as bowings and beckonings, or from ritual, such as signs of benediction and Hindu hand-postures. Dance movements convey literal and non-literal meaning. Everyday movement, he recognizes, plays an integral part in dance composition as well as in dance interpretation.

Goodman's comprehension of the *material* unifies the body, the senses, everyday movement, and dance movement. His analysis grapples with the complexity of how the parts interact, in contrast with the other aestheticians who look for simplified essences.

Participants

Since Goodman's aesthetic stance embraces complexity, he understands how one person assumes different roles in varying contexts. Unlike the other aestheticians who wrote about dance, Goodman incorporates the relationships among choreographer, dancer, and teacher in his theory, integrating their viewpoints. A notated score, for Goodman, is a connecting link, the center of these intersecting relationships among the participants. This issue is discussed fully in "The Work," below.

The Process

Though Goodman does not discuss technique *per se*, he considers how perceptual habits, styles, and ways of learning found in dance techniques are historically and culturally determined. All aspects of a culture, including techniques, he argues, are learned and practiced until they become commonplace. For example, "realism" in art is a cultural convention, and simply the name for a particular style of representation. All arts incorporate technique and composition methods which train their participants to grasp and project their artist's particular style of representation or expression in its cultural milieu.

Goodman analyzes technique, dance composition, performances, and settings as a unit: "The way we see and depict depends upon and varies with experience, practice, interests and attitudes" (10). By this he means no matter what style of dance or composition guidelines artists use, they bring their individuality to their work. Techniques for training and composing are familiar to choreographers. They can "read" them easily; that is, choreographers comprehend them. Specific techniques condition perceptual viewpoints just as dance works do. Dancers trained in one technique have perceptual habits which will color how they respond to other styles of dance. The kind of conflict embedded in different technical styles to which Goodman refers erupted recently when ballet-trained Rudolf Nureyev was featured in a dance by modern dance choreographer Martha Graham. Unaccustomed to seeing such a crossover, modern dance audiences strongly objected to this innovation. Here Goodman argues against the long-held philosophic ideas of the "innocent eye" and *tabula rasa*. People bring their own perceptual experiences to art.

Dance-art experience during a performance, Goodman asserts, is meant to be considered as an unbreakable, one-piece experience; therefore a dance composed and performed in its setting should be conceived as a totality. George Beiswanger, dance critic and theorist, terms this a "dance event" to clarify how a dance is the total unit of all its dimensions, seen and unseen.[2] Goodman's concept of the totality of the art event is like Langer's *Gestalt* response, but Langer's notion only considers the event from the audience point of view, whereas Goodman connects the viewpoints of creator, performer, and audience coequally.

Observers

Audiences need training in the skills of viewing the arts. Were they more familiar with the training and composing techniques, audiences would "read" their art experiences more easily. Audiences, Goodman argues, do not understand how art in some way remakes their world, realigns reality, and adds to their knowledge. How people experience art (or dance) depends "not only upon its orientation, distance, lighting, but upon all we know of it and upon our training, habits and concerns" (20). Within particular settings, audience response to performances will vary infinitely.

The Work

Goodman interrelates the aesthetic intention and aesthetic result of dance-art when he analyzes how a dance expresses meaning. All communication, Goodman claims, occurs by means of symbols: letters, words, text, pictures, diagrams, or gestures. In analyzing how symbols communicate, Goodman follows the traditional philosophical procedure of correcting and clarifying the theories of other aestheticians, in this case Langer. Expression and representation are two forms of denotation. They differ in this way: a picture denotes what it represents, but what it represents does not denote the picture. On the other hand, a sad picture expresses sadness, and sadness is expressed by the picture. The picture possess or exemplifies sadness. Exemplification is not always expression but all expression is exemplification. Exemplification means "is a sample of," to display but not depict or describe. In everyday nonverbal communication recognizable and meaningful gestures can denote feelings, as when shaking our head no. Gestures also can exemplify when an action is used to show how something is done, as when someone demonstrates how to do a somersault. An action or gesture might serve the purposes of denotation and exemplification at once.

Art symbols, Goodman asserts, often communicate by means of metaphor: "What is expressed is metaphorically exemplified" (85). Symbols actually but not literally possess the properties they exemplify. Goodman's concept of exemplification explains the relation between the sample and what it refers to and must be understood as relative and a matter of habit. Furthermore, these symptoms of expression, denotation, and exemplification overlap. Here Goodman corrects Langer's limited notion that the arts only express human feelings presentationally.

Goodman's analysis of the expressive properties of the arts clarifies how arts express in one or more ways. Music and dance display rhythmic patterns; both can express tranquility or tumultuous emotion and convey characteristics of movement such as heaviness. The name of a property and its expression may differ, and the aesthetic intention of the choreographer may differ from the aesthetic result in the observers.

Goodman examines how dance movements express their meaning. Dance movements, especially modern dance movements, are not part of our ordinary vocabulary of movement. The meaning they display is intrinsic to the movement and simultaneously teaches its meaning while it is done and seen: "The vocabulary evolves along with what it is used to convey" (65). The creative preferences of the choreographer determine how much literal, symbolic, or abstract movement is in any dance.

The dance itself embodies the choreographer's intention and is the basis for the aesthetic expression of the dance to the observers. After examining how dance expresses, Goodman analyzes how notation systems symbolize the unique characteristics an art (or dance) has. Because the other arts are recorded in some form of notation Goodman wondered if and how dance could be notated. He studied the dance notation system of Laban (Labanotation) long enough to determine that it satisfied his criteria for adequate notation systems. He is familiar with current arguments in the dance community about the limits of notating dance works, and his concepts resolve many of these arguments.

Goodman believes a notation system helps overcome the ephemerality of the performance arts. All art products—visual, verbal, musical, and bodily—are created by one person. If performance is necessary for the art's production and if more than the creator is necessary for its production, then a notation system addresses the limitation of time and group needs. Historically, musicians have created musical scores; playwrights, verbal scripts; poets, books of poetry; choreographers, notated scores to assist in the production of their arts.

The development of a notation system, Goodman claims, results in a "real definition" of an artwork. His analysis of the central role of notation for dance theorizing goes beyond the six comparative aestheticians who identified some of its functions for dance. Arriving at a real definition of a specific dance work involves three processes:

(1) The creator must distinguish between the properties which are part of the work, the constitutive ones, and those which may be left to the interpretation of the performers, the contingent ones.

(2) The decision concerning these properties follows contemporary informal practice, though the process of deciding what and how to notate may develop the practice.

(3) The symbols and terms must be chosen and perhaps named. This process is classificatory, and classifying "involves preferment" (32). Therefore, in the process of selecting what to symbolize in the notation system (what features of the dance to notate), choreographers establish priorities, a selection process which in turn affects the way they see their work.

Arriving at adequate symbols, Goodman holds, necessitates precise thinking. The process of choosing useful and appropriate symbols also provides terms, organized in order of importance and effect. The labels can lead to greater understanding of the work and the process of creating it. Our knowing a definition of a term, Goodman contends, is not a guarantee that we can *use* it correctly. At times only participating in the activity and having the feature of the activity labeled during the process enables one to use the term correctly. Then the terms can become verbal tools for further discourse about the material, the process, and the work of dance.

Because a notated score provides a means for distinguishing the constitutive properties of a dance-work from its contingent ones, teachers and dancers will know what parts of the dance they can personally interpret and what parts they cannot change. Because a score is a tool, it links the choreographer to the dancer, the teacher to the choreographer, the teacher to the dancer, and all of them to the dance work. The score facilitates evaluation of the performer's interpretation of the dance work and allows the work to be permanently identified and maintained over time.

Cultural Context of Dance

Goodman does not discuss history in *Languages of Art*, but his observations about the function of notation illuminate this part of the

Framework. The working out of a notation system can clarify a major problem in the writing of dance history. The scored work links performance to performance, the past to the present, and the scored dance to the performed dance. Dance historians have emphasized dancers and histories of dance productions, the *material* and the *processes*, not the works themselves, except when recounting their dramatic content. Thus the dance has appeared to be the creation of one person, when in fact dance is intimately associated with its creator only at the first stage. Once it is taught and repeated, the dance is produced by more than one person. But since few dances have been notated in a system universally accepted and taught, historians have concentrated primarily on dancers and their interpretive capabilities rather than on the dances. Concentration on the dance work, which a score provides, is new to members of the field and changes the focus from the artist to the work of art. The shift of focus may be the reason for the resistance by some creators to notating their dances. This shift from oral to written history de-emphasizes the star system and focusses on the dances themselves.

If all dances were notated, then with the use of the score the methodological problem of writing dance history might be solved. New historical accounts would integrate the dances notated in available treatises with their cultural milieu and the people who composed and performed them. Not only could art-dance be placed in its cultural perspective, but how and when a dance functions in ritual and social contexts could be more clearly understood. What dancing was done and how it was done could be meaningfully described along with who did it, when, and where.

Goodman's Ideas and Dance Theory

Goodman's analysis of the arts and their symbol systems contrasts markedly with the analyses of dance by the comparative aestheticians. Because their methods and goals differ, the comparative aestheticians identify separate characteristics of the arts, while Goodman interrelates these features and explains how they communicate. The undefined terms the aestheticians use to examine the component parts of dance are often inconsistent with dance usage and refer to intertwining features of dance. For instance, "technique," which refers to interrelated physical, emotional, expressive, and cognitive skills, applies to methods of training, teaching, composing, and performing. When Goodman sorts out features and elements of these processes in relation to each other, he operationally describes the complexities of dance's many techniques while maintaining their unity. His operational descriptions also avoid closed definitions of terms which limit understanding of dance phenomena. Goodman's effort is cohesive rather than divisive.

Goodman's thoughts about the value and function of a notation system for dance are pivotal in analyzing the problems in writing dance theory. He verifies the observations which six of the comparative aestheticians, Greene, Flaccus, Munro, Feibleman, Phenix, and Gilson, make concerning the value of a notation system for dance, but his arguments go deeper. He shows how a notation system results from in-depth thinking about dance works, and establishes a set of priorities concerning a work's permanent and interpretable features. Then too, the terminology of a notation system should be based directly on practice. These terms identify parts of the actual experience in an operational manner, eliminating the need for borrowed terms. Theoretical understanding can center on actual practice and use dance-based terms, which bridge the gap between experience and explanation.

Goodman's analysis of the role of notation reveals how the process of working out a notation system is a fundamental means to determine inductively from practice the basic values, assumptions, and goals for a theoretical explanation of dance. If the demonstrated function of notation for dance were more universally valued and taught, dance's historical past would be more directly accessible to students and scholars for performance and study in the present; relationships among the choreographer, teacher, dancer, and a dance would be more clearly articulated; and terminology would be more uniform. Notation would then contribute to analysis of dances and the related process of arriving at basic dance theory. Notation and the construction of dance theory would be understood as indispensably interdependent.

NOTES

[1] Nelson Goodman, *Languages of Art* (Indianapolis: Hackett Publishing Company, 1976), 255. Further page references to this work in this chapter will be made parenthetically in the text.

[2] George Beiswanger, "Rake's Progress or Dances and the Critic," *Dance Scope*, 10:2 (Spring-Summer 1976), 29.

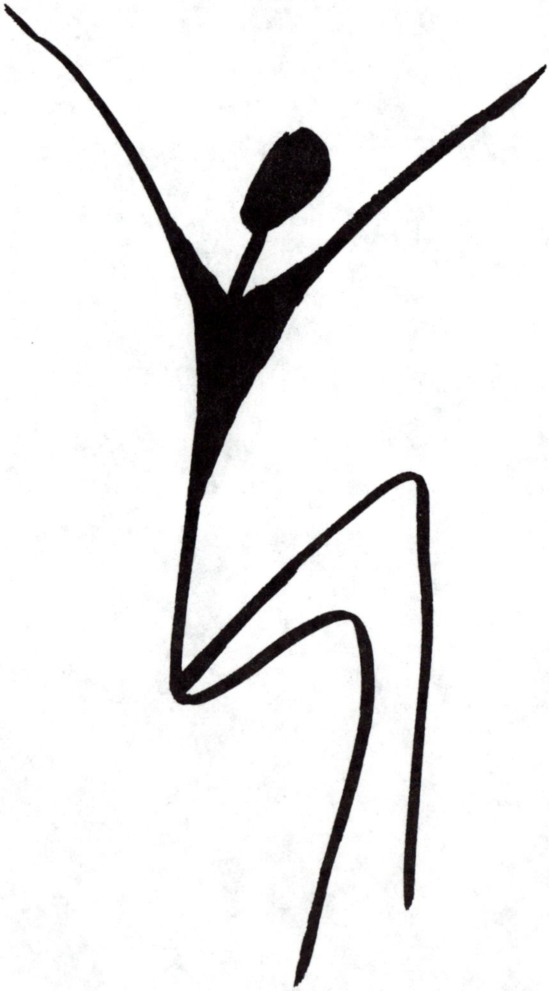

10

THE DANCE THEORY OF
RUDOLF LABAN

Rudolf Laban (1879–1958) was a dancer, choreographer, teacher, artist, and theorist who influenced several generations of dancers and dance scholars in Europe, England, and America. His dance career ranged from leading summer festivals in Ascona, Switzerland, and choreographing Dada theatrical perfomances in Vienna in the early 1920s, to directing movement choirs with factory workers in Germany in the 1930s.

Laban's dance experience generated his theoretical observations in several areas of dance. In turn, his ideas stimulated his students and colleagues to develop his ideas; the resulting movement-dance systems of theory and practice growing from this collaboration are unequalled by any other dance person in this century. He evolved a system of composition developed by Kurt Jooss and Sigurd Leeder; a system of dance notation developed by Dussia Bereska, Kurt Jooss, Albrecht Knust, and Ann Hutchinson-Guest; a system of ergonomic movement observation for human efficiency in factories, called "effort" analysis, developed with Frederic Charles Lawrence; and a method of dance education developed by Lisa Ullman, Marion North, Valerie Preston-Dunlop, Waren Lamb, Joan Russell, and Geraldine Stephenson. His ideas about the recuperative and communicative power of movement stimulated the field of dance therapy and contributed to early research in non-verbal communication.

Writing in German and then in English between 1920 and 1958, Laban published some sixteen books and thirty essays. His thinking was influenced by current scientific, psychological, anthropological, spiritual, dance, and aesthetic ideas. Nonetheless, he evolved research methods to study movement and dance, drew conclusions from his studies, and made theoretical observations from the physical activity of movement-dance itself.

Laban's writing differs from that of the other dance theorists we have analyzed. Because Laban based his conclusions on observations of dances from many countries, his understanding of these activities has universal applicability. He conceptualizes the nonverbal physical experience of dance from the united viewpoints of the creator, the observer, the physical experience, the inner source, and the actual externalized response, the dance. His explanations often include the "how" of the topic he is analyzing. Ideas other dance theorists discuss in rudimentary ways, he analyzes comprehensively.

Laban's writing about dance offers the model for evaluating the content and method of all the other writing discussed in this book because his ideas came inductively from movement experience and the practice of dance; he described these ideas in dance-derived terms. Laban's analyses thoroughly elucidate the features of and the interrelationships among the topics in the Framework. His theoretical analysis of dance demonstrates why an all-encompassing conceptualization of dance must derive from practice. He was directly involved in performing, choreographing, and teaching dance; thus he was able to identify what issues and problems need consideration, research, and clarification. Laban's dance experience and his awareness of the needs of contemporary dance stimulated him to develop a system of notation out of which grew terminology that amplified observation, execution, and analysis of dance and movement in general. His theorizing stimulated the development of dance practice in dance education, dance-movement therapy, dance ethnology, dance composition, dance research methodology, and in the related fields of non-verbal communication and industrial management. A test of the validity of dance theory is its power to inform and develop practice—this is what Laban's theoretical conceptualization of dance does.

My examination of Laban's ideas in this chapter is introductory. It is meant to reveal a more complete explanation about dance than that afforded by either the aestheticians or dance theorists, while it demonstrates why borrowing theoretical models and terminology from other fields is insufficient and unnecessary for adequate theorizing about dance. The ideas examined here are gathered from all of Laban's essays published in English from 1938 to 1961 and two of his books, *Modern Educational Dance* (1948) and *Mastery of Movement* (1960). His other books and the autobiography of his life until 1935, *A Life for Dance*, are more specialized and technical.[1] Recently Vera Maletic has published a thorough analysis of Laban's German and English writings about body, space, and expression; earlier Samuel Thornton attempted to synthesize themes found throughout Laban's writing.[2]

Laban's concept about dance reaches far beyond the concepts of Martin, Selden, and H'Doubler to include all life and all matter. The following passage exemplifies his holistic understanding of dance:

> The mighty rhythm of nature around us and the humble dance of individual creatures are closely linked by the same rule, the same fundamental form and effect. In the growth of crystals (and what is not a crystal?); in the life of plants and animals; in the characteristics of whole nations and races; in the weave of boundless existence which we call cosmos, no other driving power can be recognised but the one that also creates the dance. There are no other ways but those which are outlined in the paths and tracks of the dancing body. The infinitude of these ever-recreating forces and shapes is immeasurable and inconceivable.[3]

Matter is made up of molecules with their particles in constant motion, and thus, Laban believes, the activity and patterns of dance are related to all parts of the universe because of their common bond of patterned motion.

In *Modern Educational Dance* Laban argues for a comprehensive theory for dance which includes the complete art of movement, illustrated in the diverse study of ballet, pantomime, drama, dance in film, all forms of social dance, country and ballroom dances, games, masquerades, entertainment, ceremonies and rituals, part of oratory and speech, and work movements. The technological and mechanical effect of modern times on life, he claims, stimulated the new dance on stage, "modern dance," and produced a heightened need for movement in education and leisure. He studied movement in all its manifestations because, as he claims, "Harmony of movement in leisure time activity . . . is one of the main carriers of inner freedom and liveliness."[4] No longer a servant of humanity, movement has its own power to create states of mind frequently stronger than a person's will.

Like Martin, Laban examines why people dance. Movement binds people's lives together, enabling them to work and to take care of their daily necessities, what Laban calls "Doing." He sees people all over the world counterbalancing the movement of their doing with dancing. While this balancing of work movement with dancing is a rhythmic physical necessity, it also satisfies logical, ethical, and aesthetic human needs. Even stronger than this need to dance is the reflection of the movement patterns of our bodies' cells and the rhythmic patterns they maintain during our doing and dancing: "We are not capable of observing the bravery of our cells and their tendencies toward harmony in the same scientific manner as we do with happenings of our surroundings. But we can feel the stream and the might of noble intentions in the beneficent agitations of our muscles, in all kind of work and in the joy of dancing."[5] The rhythms of our hearts, lungs, and stomachs of which we are aware hint at more complex unseen evidence of the ongoing regular life-sustaining patterns in the cells of our bodies. Laban's understanding of cellular activity came from discoveries in physiology and microbiology. Dancing, claims Laban, is not just a social pursuit, but as vital an activity as eating, sleeping, and working.

The Material

Laban's analysis of the *material* of dance constitutes one of his major contributions to dance research because he discovered methods for observing and recording the components of body movement. He integrates the functions of the body, the senses, everyday movement, and dance movement. Unlike the other dance theorists, Laban is not compelled to demonstrate only the rational dimension of dance: "Our body together with our nervous system and all its manifestations in thought, emotion and will is in itself nothing else than a motor-process."[6]

When Laban speaks of the body, he connects its movements with the internal power which initiates them. He has a profound respect for the body: the body with its functions is the "only and absolute reality which mankind possesses."[7] The body enables people to communicate and express beliefs with distinct bodily action ranging from complete stillness to frantic motion. To illustrate the cooperation between the mobility of the body and its control, he offers an analogy of the body as the crane and the person as driver. The crane and crane-driver are a unit which—knowingly or unknowingly—follows rules of mental and bodily motion. The body cannot move without the driver, the mental controller, and the mind cannot accomplish anything without the body.[8] Laban integrates movement with the individual's internal need to move, thereby bypassing the troublesome mind-body dichotomy.

Laban does address the mind-body dualism that has plagued the history of Western philosophic thought: "When we rid ourselves of the mistaken attitude of dualism, we are apt to lose our haughty pre-occupation with the supremacy of the mind."[9] For a long time people have been unable to connect their movement with their verbal thinking. Movement thinking, he believes, organizes impressions of occurrences in one's own mind for which no words exist.

Laban suggests how pivotal the kinesthetic sense is to our awareness. It is located in our skin, conveys tactile sensation, and tells us the position of our body parts in relation to each other and in space. He thinks all the other senses are variations of the external part of kinesthesia, the sense of touch. Sound waves touch the delicate mechanisms in the ear, light waves touch the lens in the retina, odors touch the olfactory mechanisms in the nose, and flavors of food touch the taste buds.

Laban interrelates the internal stimuli of movement, called inner impulses, with everyday movement and dance movement. Every movement, transference of weight, gesture in any part of the body, Laban claims in agreement with Collingwood, reveals some feature of our inner life. Inner excitement of nerves stimulates each movement. This excitement comes from an immediate sense impression or a formerly experienced one stored in the memory. Movement displays inner impulses, the psychological and physiological impetuses for movement and the energy which sets movements in motion. Inner participation can be minimal or rich and full. The range of displayed movement patterns characterizes individual personalities. Though this idea appears to reflect an outside point of view, Laban includes the internal when he asserts that movement must be felt directly by the participant and empathetically in the muscles of the observer.

Weight, time, space, and flow are the components of all movement. They become personal characteristics when the moving person takes an attitude toward them, such as the choice between a pat and a slap. The dynamic variations of movement can be analyzed, described, and controlled by understanding these components. The study of the dynamics of movement is central to Laban's classification of movement and is among his major contributions to a theoretical understanding of dance movement. Laban's analysis of the components goes far beyond the other dance theorists who only identify time, space, and force. Laban adds weight and calls force "flux" or "flow" (and later "effort"). "Effort" is the link between the internal need to move and its outer visible resulting movement. His ideas about classifying movement and his descriptive terms connect the internal urge to move with the external result in actual movement and thus explain the *material* of dance in significantly greater depth than the other writers we have examined.

The reasons why people move provide source material for dance movement. Tangible and logical reasons motivate work and work-related activities; intangible and irrational reasons stimulate prayer, worship, and art. Movement, he contends, reveals a state of mind and is influenced by the environment of the mover. Group movement shows a desire to get in touch with another person. Laban believes human beings have an "inner urge to move in harmony with the source of life and actually with the whole of the universe."[10] To Laban all dance is natural.

Laban integrates the inner and outer sources of movement: "The synthesis of our internal and external movements is the central function from which all actions derive, with their causes, consequences and aims."[11] The common denominator of work and play activities is movement. Both kinds of movement are directed by thought and emotion (condensed into the concept "mind"); both originate in the human drive for inner fulfillment, the human need to externalize products of the imagination which take the form of dreams and fantasies. Therefore, movement must be understood as a partnership between the real world of people and their dream world. Laban synthesizes the materials of dance: dance and work have movement in common, and dance movement is influenced by work movement. In work, the mind (thought and emotion) directs the movement, whereas in play and dance, movement stimulates the activity of the mind.

Participants

When Laban refers to the people who participate in the dance experience, he rarely uses the words "artist" or "choreographer." He believes no clear distinction exists between the producing and reproducing artist. He does distinguish between the professional and non-professional dancer: "The dancer dances for himself, sometimes with others, very rarely for others. The latter is a professional dancer."[12] Laban's concept of "dancer" is universal and includes all people who dance social, folk, or ritual dances:

> A dancer is moved by ideal considerations in the multiple change of his positions; and each of these changes is always done in a definite rhythm. He moves not only from place to place, but also from mood to mood. The recovery value of this free activity is incontestable.[13]

In these three sentences, Laban connects the material of dance (rhythmic changes of position and places in spaces), the process of dancing (motion from place to place), the reasons for dancing (mood changes), and the result (its recovery value). His writing provides a model for a theoretical consideration of dance because it encompasses the interconnections and complex multiple dimensions of the many features of dance.

The Process

Laban's understanding of the components of movement and the common features shared by technique, composition, and performance enables him to analyze the what, the content of these parts of dance-making, and the how, the method of producing dances. His analysis continually connects dance movement to its sources: inner impulses and everyday movement.

For Laban, technique derives from a person's natural faculty of "becoming aware of the patterns which his effort impulses create and of learning to develop, to reshape and to use them."[14] The appearance of effortless skill is a common characteristic of laborers and virtuoso performers, he observes; both share the inner urge to move and the goal to acquire expert facility in specific movements.

In *Modern Educational Dance* Laban defines free dance technique as having no preconceived, prescribed style. Technique training, he argues, should be based on the exploration of movement in terms of space, time, weight, and force to increase the richness of the "effort" life of dancers. He presents "Sixteen Basic Movement Themes" and the "Rudiments of Free Dance Techniques"[15] to stimulate students and teachers to discover the widest range of movement possibilities for dance. The themes include movement problems of increasing complexity, exploring combinations of space, time, weight, and force. Here is an example of the movement exploration he recommends: find movements which are variations of light and heavy weight at low level, moving only side to side. Laban's techniques increase the ability of students to improvise with freedom and potentially endless variety.

Perfected technique can be described in terms of the major components of movement and indicates an inner attitude (conscious or unconscious) toward these factors. For instance, flow is "free," "bound," or has degrees in between. The parts of the body used influence the flow as does the choice of bodily actions, such as limbs gathering (gestures start away from the body and come in) or limbs scattering (gestures start near the body and go away). These components can be used by teachers and choreographers to analyze and describe dance or work movements. Laban's understanding of movement is useful both for generating new movement and examining it once it is formed.

Laban clarifies what part feelings play in composition. Feelings are physical and emotional: "Our physical orientation in the world, our intuitive awareness of mass motion (Weight, Space, Time and Flow), restraint and autonomy and all characteristic feeling that goes with it, are probably the preeminent subject-matter of the dance."[16] The real incentive for any kind of dance comes from the dramatic elements of action life. The raw material of movement ideas are steps and gestures which people use expressively in chains of action. What choreographers feel and what movements they choose to represent their feelings are quite different because like play, dance has rules. These rules emerge from within the dancemaking process, where they have great freedom in how to apply them.

The major kinds of dance Laban analyzes, group and solo, integrate real action, self-expression, and symbolic action. The contents of a dance emerge from a physical satisfaction or dissatisfaction in performing particularly shaped movements with certain parts of the body. Contrast is crucial: being in space or fighting it, indulging time or fighting it. Laban suggests "such contrasts" constitute "the art of dancing."[17] Laban's concept of contrast as the crucial feature of art is more specific than H'Doubler's notion of rhythm as its basis.

Why does someone make a dance? Going beyond Selden, Martin, and H'Doubler, Laban claims inspiration can come from movement improvisation or from within one's mind, but like the others he warns against only an intellectual construction. The felt need to make a dance is similar to the need to make any artwork. Movement, the essential characteristic of life, reveals feeling-generated gestures which are the source of movement in art-dance. Thus as Selden asserted, echoing her teacher Laban, internal rhythms conduct dance.

Laban describes the techniques of performance in personal and general terms. Performing provides self-realization for a person by allowing him or her to enter "into a relationship with the great principles of movement harmony in nature."[18] Performance incorporates concentration, meditation, and contemplation. These general characteristics arise naturally and are necessary for the dancer to have the power to stir an audience.

The performer's unique efforts affect the way audiences will respond to a performance. A person who relates well to space, observes Laban, has mastery of attention. A person with mastery of weight has intention, and a person who has mastered time has decision (MM, 85). Effort shadings, which Laban calls "Action Drives," are not only seen and heard; they are also kinesthetically understood by audience members, thereby conveying the power of the performer's internal message. Laban's analysis of dance performance integrates the viewpoints of the performer and the audience.

All of the arts are interrelated because they convey human expressiveness. Music, thinks Laban, "heightens rhythmical components of bodily movement and partly translates their emotional content into sound waves" (MM, 8). Laban studied patterns of movement to see if movement scales existed the way sound scales do. He formulated the movement scales he found as "Space Harmony." The study of "Space Harmony" includes exploring a wide range of spatial forms and learning sequences of movement which feel to the moving body as logical as musical scales sound to our Western ears. He claims an amazing correspondence exists between sound and movement patterns.

Laban's consideration of the topics in the *process* is thorough: he includes the internal and external viewpoints, the physical, emotional, and cognitive sides of the topics, and analyzes the connections among all of them. In these explanations, he uses physically defined dance-based terms.

Observers

What happens in the theater, Laban argues, happens between the poles of a magnetic current connecting the audience and performers. Performances function on two levels: the entertainment level where the audience gains comfort and relief from their daily lives, and the deeper more complex level requiring inner participation of the audience in which the performance mirrors a person's inner being. In a good performance, the mind of the observer is powerfully submerged by the flow of constantly changing happenings. If the observer concentrates with sincere inner participation, then no time exists for the elaborate thought or contemplation possible when one views non-performing art—a picture, a piece of sculpture, or a magnificent building. Laban's grasp of how audience members participate in a theater performance applies as well to non-performing participants in ritual dance and to the dancers in social dance who are simultaneously performers and observers.

The Work

Laban offers a few simple definitions of a dance: stylized play not directly related to dramatic "effort" behavior, or the poetry of bodily actions in space. When he explains what is in a dance, he conveys its complex dimensionality more fully. In a passage in *Mastery of Movement* Laban includes the following parts in the "gliding and surging" of a dance: the tense "stillness of anticipation"; the "many actions of stir"; the repeated "will to act"; polaric forces separating and reuniting; their symbolic form and structure; the strength which builds the created composition

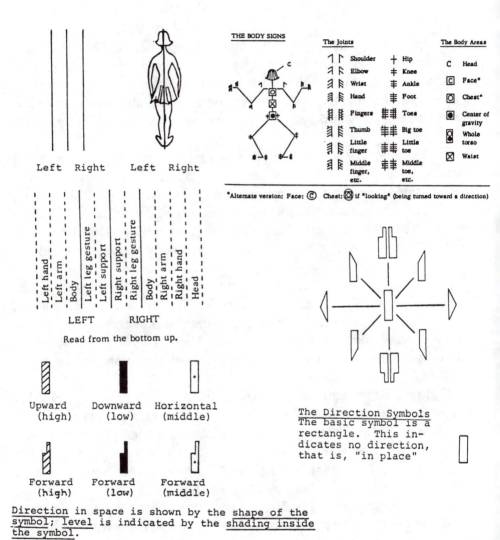

Left   Right   Left   Right

THE BODY SIGNS

The Joints

	Shoulder	Hip
	Elbow	Knee
	Wrist	Ankle
	Hand	Foot
	Fingers	Toes
	Thumb	Big toe
	Little finger	Little toe
	Middle finger, etc.	Middle toe, etc.

The Body Areas

C   Head
C   Face*
O   Chest*
●   Center of gravity
     Whole torso
⊠   Waist

*Alternate version: Face: Ⓒ   Chest: Ⓞ if "looking" (being turned toward a direction)

Left hand | Left arm | Body | Left leg gesture | Left support | Right support | Right leg gesture | Body | Right arm | Right hand | Head

LEFT   RIGHT

Read from the bottom up.

Upward (high)   Downward (low)   Horizontal (middle)

Forward (high)   Forward (low)   Forward (middle)

Direction in space is shown by the shape of the symbol; level is indicated by the shading inside the symbol.

The Direction Symbols
The basic symbol is a rectangle. This indicates no direction, that is, "in place"

FIGURE 1. The Symbols of Labanotation

in time; the dancer's merged grace, nobility, conscience, and behavior; and the mysterious physical melody that uplifts the core of life (*MM*, 31-32). A dance is an entity for Laban. It has cognitive, emotional, and physical motivation and content; it is shaped by rhythmic and muscular energy and texture; it has bodily and symbolic content which communicates physical meaning.

Laban analyzes how a dance communicates the aesthetic intention of a dancer or choreographer. Any mood is conveyed through several components: the directions the movements take and the shapes they create, rhythmic development of a sequence of movements, the tempo in which the entire dance is executed, and the placement of accents and organization of phrases. The physical, visible features, Laban asserts, convey the aesthetic message of a dance.

A well made dance, claims Laban, is made up of contrasts related to the basic "fight or flight" response of people. Thus these movement ideas, as a dance, produce in the spectator an experience of the inner tensions displayed by the dancer dancing the dance. Dance awakens deep stirrings within the unconscious functions of the minds of spectators and performers alike.

Laban's major contribution to the development of dance theory is his notation system. He claims he had to invent it to help people remember their dances in the schools, movement choirs, factories, and therapeutic settings in which he worked. His system, known as Labanotation in the United States and Kinetography Laban in Europe, records any movement in symbols. The same symbols are used for all parts of the body in vertical columns on graph paper. Starting at the center where the body weight is placed, the direction, level, and tempo of the movements of the entire body are visible at once. (See fig. 1.) Learning to read the basic symbols takes only a few minutes and learning enough detail to read notation, a few months. The dance is recorded on a score which enables anyone to reproduce it entirely (fig. 2). Laban also developed a way to analyze and record the energy dimension of movement in what is called "effort" analysis. Together, these notation systems deal with the substance and spirit of human movement.

A notation system, Laban argues, is as necessary for dance as for music and poetry. The visible patterns can be described in words, but

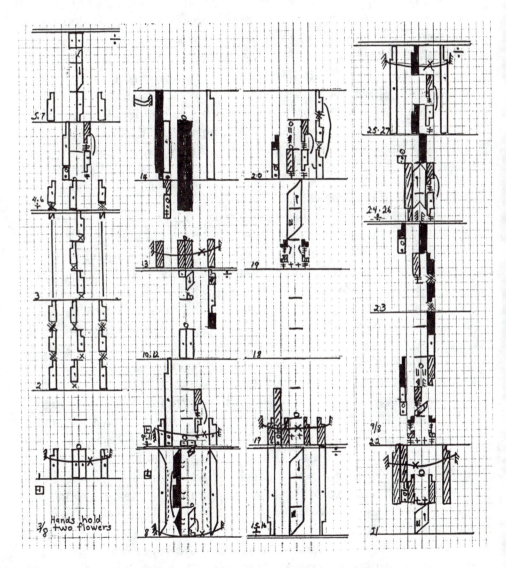

FIGURE 2. "Mariner Man" dance score in Labanotation

dance's deeper meaning is inexpressible verbally. Recording movement patterns in appropriate symbols replaces the need to translate a dance into words, which are non-physical verbal symbols. Inadequate word-substitutes from the terminology of psychology, Laban argues, may be dispensed with so that "dance-movements will be recognised as entities of their own. while analogies or similarities with national or historical movement characteristics might still play a secondary role in their registration."19 Note Laban's conception here of dance movements as entities. The process of notating a dance makes a record of the ephemerality of a dance in performance. Notation, Laban realizes, will increasingly have a role in the study of dance.

The Functions of the Process

The activity of making and performing dances has educational and therapeutic impact on people of all ages. Dance, Laban argues, acts as a harmonizing influence in education by balancing physical and verbal instruction. These streams of instruction contrast intensely like the ebb and flow of tides; dance can offer a soothing influence on the conflict. This power of active dancing to balance school activities and provide movement education as recreation has been recognized around the world for centuries.

In *Modern Educational Dance* Laban gives several reasons why creative dance is important for children: to strengthen and exercise their spontaneous urge to move, to preserve this spontaneity, to foster artistic expression, and to integrate intellectual knowledge with creative ability. The long-term benefits can last for a lifetime, enabling people to feel united with nature and to balance the processes of living. Creative dance helps balance the cognitive and the feeling parts of one's self, and it unites the waking and the dream life. Inner integration, he fears, degenerates easily, so the major task of the dance educator is to re-awaken and strengthen this capability in students.

Dance indeed has therapeutic power, but proper study and use of movement education can even be preventive. Laban believes dance therapy is the most fundamental branch of art therapy; it works by balancing mechanical and mental training with motor experience. Dance produces harmonious and disharmonious sensations, which open a dancing person to a deep experience of inner concentration. Then emotional life and rational experience link, at least for the moment: "inner health and balance . . . accompany the improvement of organic functions."[20] For Laban, "inner health" is found in new forms of mental mobility which accompany rehabilitation. Laban's perspective on movement expression helped launch the field of dance therapy in which several of his students or those of Mary Wigman such as Trudi Schoop, Lilyan Espenak, Mary Whitehouse, and Elizabeth Polk, have become leaders.

The Functions of the Work

Laban's understanding of the functions of dance in human culture is broad, yet he is sensitive to the complexity of the roles dance plays in specific cultures. He distinguishes among the *art* of dancing for expression and entertainment, dance *education* for learning our cultural movement vocabulary, and the *science* of dance for the study of dance and its relation to human endeavor. He believes tribal or national dances are created through the repetition of "effort" configurations characteristic of the community in which they are done: their educational function enables children to learn the habits, customs, worship, and religious practices of their forebears. Such dances give pleasurable aid to work and facilitate rhythmic teamwork. They contribute richness to ceremonial practices: "In dancing, or movement-thinking, man first became aware of a certain order in his higher aspirations towards spiritual life" (*MM*, 18).

Ballroom, country, and folk dances are enjoyed by people around the world for social and recreational purposes because they permit people to exhibit forms of exaltation. The dances embody their community's cultural values and reflect the current status of movement. The social dances of today, Laban observes, with their few unimaginative steps, reflect the mechanical, repetitious lives which people live and indicate low respect for movement art.

The art of movement, Laban asserts, is an almost self-contained discipline which speaks for itself and mostly in its own idiom. The art of movement is, however, not isolated from its other functions. Dance can be appreciated and enjoyed either as a spectacle performed by professionals or as a recreational activity performed by laypersons. This distinction between kinds of entertainment is arbitrary and unusual for Laban, who most often sees the interconnections and overlap of these dance functions. He clarifies this distinction when he says, "The art of dancing in which a person or a group seeks, beyond entertainment, a kind of self expression leads further to the art of movement in which the realisation of our unity with nature is attempted and found."21   Art, although entertaining, goes further than spectacular and recreational dance by enabling dancers and members of the audience to feel the ongoing harmony of universal motion.

For Laban, the movement of dance is basic to life. Dancing is the essential counterbalancing experience to Doing, and it binds people to their communities. The connection between a person's mind and cell-state must not be interrupted because the person is then no longer sensitive to what is happening in the community. Laban claims the function of dance as a means of human bonding is universal, ongoing, and true for any form of dance.

The Material Studied

From Laban's perspective, the theoretical basis of standard kinesiology is insufficient because it uses a mechanistic model based on laws derived from the motional properties of inanimate objects. The behavior of inanimate and animate objects is different; animate ones have the ability to control the flow of their movement. This inner "effort" function, Laban believes, must be studied along with mechanical functions.

Beyond training people to observe movement accurately, Laban points to the necessity of studying the synchrony of the external, observable movements with the internal mobility of our cells in their assembled shapes and molecular pathways. No boundary exists between the mobility of our cells and our bodies because they are indivisible. The same rules that apply to our bodies and cells, Laban asserts, govern the movement of atoms, crystals, stars, organic growth, and human consciousness. The study of dance movement also requires the study of humanity's inner life where movement and action originate. If understood, dance can be the doorway to our humanity.

The Process Studied

The academic field of dance is in its early stages of development; therefore, much of it has yet to be systematically studied. Laban's theoretical insights support systematic research. The inner urge to dance, Laban insists, must be the priority for research. Understanding what lies behind the tensions, anticipations, and fulfillments in a dancer's choice of movements, he argues, is a necessary prerequisite of any scientific research into dance.

Laban's study of dance movement led him to explore all kinds of movement, including that of factory workers. From such broad knowledge, he concluded that the human drive to perfect movement skills is universal. The study of movement techniques deals with how one masters the individual movements required for an activity. Dance technique, he claims, is useful for systematic movement education of the dancer, but technique is not dance. The techniques of older, "historical" forms of dance should also be studied because they give insight into the spirit of the times when they flourished.

The Work Studied

Throughout his writings, Laban reflects on the cultural context of dance. His comments integrate anthropological and historical approaches to conceptualizing past events and experiences. He understands history from an unusual perspective: "It took centuries after centuries until it was realised that the joy and misery of certain epochs of human history were intimately connected with the attitude of the people living at the times towards movement."[22] The academic discipline of history uses the written record as source material to study and analyze the past. Since movement has been inadequately recorded, this factor has been overlooked by historians until Laban and other scholars interested in the body and movement sciences, especially anthropologists, uncovered this hidden part of humanity's past.[23]

Laban places all human endeavor into the moving universe. What appears to be static reality, observes Laban, is motion arrested. He believes "primitive" people were sensitive to nature's rhythms and valued the alternating urges of doing and dancing. When these people began to elaborate upon their urge to dance, Laban argues, what we know as civilization began to develop. Now dance has rare historical significance and is regarded as one of the valued and admired outgrowths of civilized life: "The functioning of the human mind would not be what it is without the arts; Dance is the primary art of man."24   The study of great epochs, works, and choreographers, Laban contends, gives us insight into the contribution dance has made to culture. Dance reflects the dignity of life; when dancing has lost its significance as inner expression, popular values have degenerated to the level of only satisfying superficial desires.

Dances of different historical periods, Laban claims, reflect the needs and events of those periods. For instance, he claims that Noverre found peasant and court dance unsuitable for people during the development of industrial society. When Isadora Duncan performed lyric, rather than dramatic, dances in a free-flowing costume, she responded to the growing freedom for women in the 1910s and 1920s. Laban believes our contemporary "modern" dance, with its richer innovative techiques and freely structured forms of composition, reflects modern times.

Our current technical cultural environment, he contends, is lopsided. Yet a growing awareness has led scholars in several fields to the systematic study of the function and value of movement in human life. Laban has contributed much to this awareness in such areas as work efficiency programs in factories, dance therapy for prison inmates, creative dance as the basis for teaching all the arts to children, and the cross-cultural study of space and gesture.

Laban's Dance-Based Theory

Laban's conceptualization of dance goes beyond the need to notate dances to humanity's need to dance. He examines the inner urge to move as part of life, distinguishes the need to move in daily life from the need to dance, and identifies the range of efforts and unconscious drives that dance satisfies. Dance as art is only one function he analyzes. The art form itself is put in its contexts: personal, social, cultural, psychological, and universal.

Laban's theoretical interpretation of dance passes the test of good theory. His explication stems from practice, fits all forms, uses, and styles of dance over time, elucidates practice of dance in education, therapy, and composition, and stimulates research focussing on movement analysis in dance, sport, physical therapy, and industry. His method of deriving theory also provides dance researchers with a model. Laban started his study of dance by dancing, by practicing traditional and new styles of technique, and by choreographing. From this base he followed a multi-disciplinary path which led him inward to human psychology and physiology and outward to matter, organic and inorganic, and then to movements of work and play in cultures around the world, past and present.

The material of dance—the body moving in space and time—is the common element Laban examined and this led him to study the structure of cells, stars, and all movement in between. His thinking places dance events in their context and connects the parts to a whole. His world view is holistic; he sees unity and connectedness where others see separation and isolation. He discovered the movement component in our lives, identified it as an entity, and through his detailed and precise understanding of movement, symbolized it in notation and effort analysis. Thus while maintaining a comprehensive view of the field of dance, Laban has produced theories of space usage and movement and effort analysis; further, his ideas stimulated colleagues, students, and other researchers to explore other components of movement and dance.

Laban's writings have few of the shortcomings of the other aestheticians and dance theorists we have studied. He writes from many integrated and identified viewpoints, offers definitions of his terms with physical examples to illustrate his ideas and applies no unsubstantiated conceptual models from other fields to dance. His dance-based ideas deepen intrinsic understanding of dance for members of the dance community, and his discoveries are increasingly valued by scholars in other fields.

NOTES

1 Rudolf Laban and F. C. Lawrence, *Effort* (London: Macdonald and Evans, 1947); Laban, *Choreutics*, ed. Lisa Ullman (London: Macdonald and Evans, 1966).

2 Vera Maletic, *Body—Space—Expression* (Berlin: Mouton de Gruyter, 1987); and Samuel Thornton, *Laban's Theory of Movement* (Boston: Plays, Inc., 1971).

3 Rudolf Laban, "The Aesthetic Approach to the Art of Dancing," *Laban Art of Movement Guild Magazine* [*LAMGM*], 23 (1959), 29.

4 Rudolf Laban, "What Has Led You to Study Movement?" *LAMGM*, 7 (1951) 7.

5 Rudolf Laban, "The Importance of Dancing," *LAMGM*, 22 (1959); rpt. in *Rudolf Laban Speaks About Movement and Dance* [*RLSMD*] ed. Lisa Ullman (London: Laban Art of Movement Centre, 1971), 16.

6 Rudolf Laban, "The Rhythm of Living Energy," *LAMGM*, 22 (1959), 44.

7 Rudolf Laban, "Extract from an Address Held by Mr. Laban on a Meeting for Community-Dance in 1936," *LAMGM*, 52 (1974), 6.

8 Rudolf Laban, "Education Through the Arts," *LAMGM*, 19 (1957), in *RLSMD*.

9 Laban, "Importance," *RLSMD*, 20.

10 Laban, "Importance," 16.

11 Laban, "Extract," 7.

12 Laban, "Aesthetic Approach," 29.

13 Rudolf Laban, "The Rhythm of Effort and Recovery, Part II," *LAMGM*, 24 (1960), 13.

14 Rudolf Laban, *The Mastery of Movement* (London: Macdonald and Evans, 1960), 17. Further references to this book in this chapter will be cited paranthetically in the text preceded by *MM*.

15 Rudolf Laban, *Modern Educational Dance* (London: Macdonald and Evans, 1948), 25-84.

16 Rudolf Laban, "Dance and Symbol," *LAMGM*, 22 (1959), 28.

17 Laban, "The Rhythm of Effort," 15.

18 Laban, "Education," 5.

19 Rudolf Laban, "Meaning," *LAMGM*, 22 (1959), 31.

20 Laban, "The Rhythm of Living Energy," 45.

21 Laban, "Education," 5.

22 Rudolf Laban, "Laban Lecture, 1957," *LAMGM*, 18 (1957), 7.

23 See Jonathan Benthall and Ted Polhemus, *Body as a Medium of Exp‐ression* (London: Allen Lane, 1975); Ted Polhemus, ed., *The Body Reader* (New York: Pantheon Books, 1978); and D. W. Winnicott, *Playing and Reality* (London: Penguin Books, 1982).

24 Laban, "Importance of Dancing," 12.

11

GENERATING DANCE THEORY FROM
DANCE-BASED EXPERIENCE

The meaning of "dance theory" is tangled and many-layered. Dance writers use "theory" when they refer to a single explanation of a part of the field, such as a theory of dance criticism; at other times they use "theory" not as a single idea but as a collection of guiding principles. All of the writers analyzed in this book use "theory" as a collective noun to mean a comprehensive explanation of the practice of all dimensions of dance and as guidelines for understanding the field of dance.

Dance practitioners cloud the meaning of "dance theory" when in conversation they use "theory" in several sometimes contradictory ways. Dance faculty use the term as an adjective when they refer to their non-studio classes as "theory" classes. When our colleagues in music departments hear this usage they assume "theory" classes are, like theirs, composition classes; "Twelve Tone Theory" is one of several composition theories music students study. In common speech the noun "theory" means an ideal, even unrealistic, explanation of a phenomenon and is the opposite of practice, yet scientists accept a theory as "true" until a more accurate one is found to explain observable features of the world.

Several dance writers have explicitly addressed the question "What is dance theory?"—among them John Martin, dance critic George Beiswanger, dancer and choreographer Merce Cunningham, and dancer and educator Gertrude Lippincott. These dance writers address the issue but disagree about what constitutes "dance theory" and from whence it derives.

In 1933, John Martin proclaimed: "The only source of enlightenment has been the actual performances of the dancers themselves. In the last analysis this is the only reliable source to be sure, for all theory which is more than hypothetical must be deduction from the practice of the best

artists."[1]   For Martin the source of theory is practice; its purpose is to
lessen artists' confusion about dance as an art and enlighten audiences beyond actual dance performances.

Lippincott's 1949 call for a more fully developed dance theory carries
an emphasis different from Martin: "This need for theoretical writing is
felt by audiences and artists . . . to help in interpretation and understanding of the various forms of dance." Such theory, she argued, had not yet
developed "a systemized group of principles and definitions. . . .
Theoretical analysis has been notably lacking."[2] Lippincott shares Martin's purpose for theory; but for her, it is a set of principles separate from
practice.

Cunningham, innovator of the "chance" method of composing
dances, became a spokesman for "anti-intellectualism" in dance. In 1955,
he indirectly described his definition of dance theory and its function when
he asserted:

> So we don't, it seems to me, have to worry ourselves about
> providing relationships and continuities and orders and
> structures—they cannot be avoided. They are the nature of
> things. They are ourselves and our materials and our envi-
> ronment. If a dancer dances—which is not the same as hav-
> ing theories about dancing . . . everything is there. The
> meaning is there, if that is what you want.[3]

Cunningham views theory as ever-changing relationships, continuities,
orders, and structures which do not necessarily clarify the meaning of
dance. Knowledge about dance (theory), for Cunningham, derives from
doing and seeing it.

The writing and thinking about dance of Beiswanger dates back to
1935. In his analysis of the nature of theorizing he identifies choreographers who make dances, critics who comment on them, and aestheticians who theorize with regard to both. These specialities, he claims, do
not require a break between thinking and doing, because dance-making
requires a special intelligence while dance-viewing is more than just gathering impressions: "Dance theorizing does not bear fruit unless rooted in
dance doings and viewings." Like Martin, Beiswanger claims theory is
based on the dance in performance. Theory is derived from dances, which

"have reasons for being what they are; they exhibit the theory of these reasons in practice; and they demonstrate the aesthetics of the theory in operation."[4] Combining the views of Martin and Cunningham, Beiswanger thinks dance theory comes from dances, choreographers, and writers whose joint efforts circumscribe dance events.

Theory for Martin and Beiswanger is a general set of principles offered to explain dance reality and is derived from actual experience of dance. For Lippincott and Cunningham, it is the ideal, general, and abstract set of principles used to compare and judge dance events. These dance writers do not entirely agree on the source or the function of dance theory. Disagreement in an academic field is a sign of intellectual vitality, but the importance of theory-making and testing necessitates clarifying this basic issue. Until the recent growing awareness of the value of Laban's ideas, the dance community has looked to aestheticians to provide the field of dance with theoretical constructs.

Dance Notation and Dance Theory

Though Martin, Selden, and the aestheticians Greene, Flaccus, Munro, Feibleman, Phenix, Gilson, and Goodman referred to the need for notation to record dances, none foresaw its full theoretical ramifications. Since notating a dance provides a score, the score then defines a dance as an entity. Goodman's description of why a notation system is necessary for formulating dance theory grew out of studying the notation system of Laban. The depth, breadth, clarity, and rich complexity of Laban's theoretical understanding of dance resulted, in part, from the process of formulating his notation system. His work begins to reach the theoretical understanding Martin, Selden, Goodman, and the six comparative aestheticians suggest and that other scholars are discovering can be generated by using notation as a research tool.

The quest to record dances goes back at least 3,000 years. The many notation systems devised were geared to the style and function of the dances being notated. Before this century, many of the books of dance theory contained mostly notated dances with minimal introductory theoretical background. Throughout history, dances have been recorded for several reasons: for teaching dances to students, publicizing a class or teacher, documenting a dance for an archive, or commemorating an occa-

sion for posterity.   One notation system often can be translated into another, and dances described in words may be rewritten in notation, placed
side by side for comparison, and studied. In the past twenty years dance
scholars have awakened to the value of notating dances for research purposes: dance notation allows us to compare and contrast structures, mo-
tifs, movement vocabularies, the use of the body, and different styles of
performing the same movements.   For example, Maria Drabecka's
notated samples show, among other things, "that the older *cinque passi*
were danced on the spot, the later steps rather forwards"[5] (see fig. 1).

Recently, dance notation experts have written about the research
potential of notation for developing the body of knowledge of dance. With
several competing systems of notation in use (Labanotation, Benesch,
Eshkol-Wachmann), the inventors and users of notation agree on its major
characteristics and functions even though they disagree on the exact way
to symbolize the movements because each notation system conceptualizes
movement from a different point of view. This variety does not impede
research; on the contrary, as Lucy Venable points out, the variations enrich
our understanding of movement the way the multiplicity of verbal languages facilitates expression of the wide range of human thought communicated in words.[6]

Notation functions to document dances and dance material for re-
peating, archiving, and studying specific dances. These functions relate to
the *work*, but notation facilitates analysis of the *material* and *process* as
well. Several scholars (among them Ann Hutchinson-Guest, Muriel
Topaz, and Jill Beck) point out how teaching dance technique can be en-
hanced by having students study books of notated dance technique. Topaz
describes another benefit of notation, describing a symposium on movement with notators and medical practitioners in which the notators were
far more perceptively and accurately able to analyze detailed movement
than their "scientific" counterparts.[7]

Choreographers who use notation while they compose a dance report how notating their work has deepened and broadened their creative
processes.[8] Even during the sometimes tedious process of learning how to
read and write notation, students report a marked increase in their understanding of movement and a heightened awareness of the range of potential movements they have available for their compositions. Thus both the

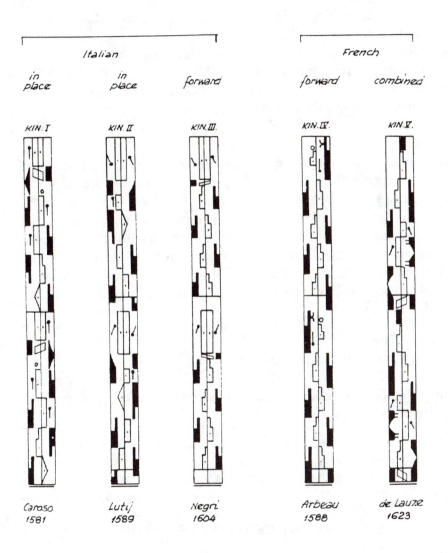

FIGURE 1. An example of research results using Labanotation:
Cinque passi in dance treatises from 1581 to 1623

process of notating and its product, the score, can increase understanding of many dimensions of dance: creative, pedagogical, critical, analytical, historical, and contextual.

By studying Labanotation, Goodman is able to analyze and explain the value of notation for dance thinking. The process of formulating the symbols of dance notation, Goodman believes, requires a fundamental theoretical analysis of the work, a real dance. In this process the notator-choreographer automatically establishes artistic or expressive priorities when deciding what properties of a dance to record and what to leave for individual interpretation. Though influenced by cultural, aesthetic, and personal criteria, this identification of priorities is based on study of the dance itself, and therefore establishes a viable definition of a dance from which, Laban and Goodman think, all theoretical explanations are derived. In sum, the lack of a widely used notation system for dance has extensive negative theoretical ramifications. Notation of dances provides the field of dance with a major research tool to study the actual substance and subject of the field of dance—dances—and not just the ideas of other scholars about dance.

Testing Dance Theory

Although notation documents a dance, it is only one part of a complex activity needing theoretical delineation. The following is an operational definition of comprehensive dance theory which is derived from direct practice of and experience in dance:

> Comprehensive dance theory can encompass and explain all dimensions of dance practice. It is valid over time, fits all forms, uses, styles of dance, elucidates practice, and generates further development of the field. Dance-derived terms are used to explain dance phenomena, and these terms are operationally defined and physically understandable.

This definition of comprehensive dance theory serves as an evaluative criterion for assessing the *adequacy, comprehensiveness, accuracy,* and *clarity* of the dance theory in this study.

Dance theory needs to be tested for its *adequacy.* How adequate the writing is depends on the technical terms, conceptual models, range of topics, and identified interrelationships. The adequacy of the dance theory determines how well it informs its readers, both dancers and non-dancers. The adequacy of the writing of four dance theorists in this study was tested by examining how fourteen aestheticians interpreted their works.

Is the writing of the dance theorists *comprehensive*? The explanations of dance need to incorporate historical, ethnological, educational, social, compositional, and artistic sides of dance practice. The dance theorists analyzed demonstrate, though they do not state, that a theoretical examination of dance requires conceptualizing the domain of dance by integrating its historical, comparative, and systematic aspects.

Disciplinary sources of thinking and conceptual models decisively influence the *accuracy* of the theoretical discussions of dance. If the source of thinking about dance theory is dance practice, and if the conceptual approach emerges from dance, as is the case with Laban, then the theoretical explanations are likely to describe dance activities accurately. If dance is made to fit into conceptual approaches from other disciplines and is explained in terms used in outdated theory from other fields, then dance is distorted or shortchanged. This is the major problem I have identified. The theoretical explanations of Selden, Martin, and H'Doubler are partly inaccurate because they are incomplete. Their concentration on the expressive-communicative part of dance diminishes the importance of the source of that communication, the dance itself.

The terms and definitions used by the dance theorists determine the *clarity* of their explanations of dance. The aestheticians who used their books as source material used the same or similar terms. Both groups of theorists discuss complex and abstract issues in terms which, in the field of dance and the field of philosophy, remain essentially jargon. Both groups of writers offer few operational definitions of terms such as "movement," "space," and "body," since they assume readers understand these words. Because the dance theorists left key terms undefined, the ideas these words sketch remain vague and non-physical.

This vagueness is compounded by their lack of concrete examples and their reliance on unsubstantiated generalizations. Though theoretical writing is general by design, examples are needed to clarify general principles. The dearth of verbal or pictorial illustrations in the writings of the dance theorists and aestheticians limits their ideas to an often ambiguous level of abstraction. A telling example of this vague abstraction is the definitions of dance in the analyses by the eleven aestheticians (p. 98). Since the aestheticians used the writings of the dance theorists as their sources of information, this lack of clarity is partly due to the abstract and over-general explanations and undefined jargon of the dance theorists.

A telling pattern emerges in the material we have analyzed. Goodman's multi-dimensional description of dance in the context of his study of notation and the symbol systems of art reflects the depth and clarity of Laban's analysis of dance. Compared to Goodman, the analyses of dance by the other thirteen aestheticians, regardless of their aesthetic insights and conceptual premises, lack depth. This deficiency stems in part from the dance theoretical sources used by the aestheticians. The dance authors did not adequately explain the physical reality of the dance entity which must be the central focus of dance thinking.

Dance scholar and Laban student Janet Adshead has recently written two books applying Laban's movement analysis of time and space to the contexts of art, ritual, and social dance in choreography, performance, criticism, and historical and anthropological dance literature. She and her colleagues have further developed this method of analysis for components, forms, performances, and evaluations of dance to enable students to be tested in the subject matter of dance on General Certificate of Education examinations in England and Wales.[9] The depth and range of the methodological guidelines put forward in Adshead's books is dance-based and comes directly from the influential work of Laban.

Toward a Research Paradigm for the Field of Dance

In academic practice, theories emerge from a systematic study of a subject. The research methods used to study a subject are guided by an accepted research paradigm—those ideas, parameters, and goals for a given field upon which members of that field agree. The paradigm or model for guiding research is often implicit in the thinking and writing of members of the field. The researchers who make up this community of scholars trust their intertwined theoretical and methodological system of beliefs. It provides the basis for their selection, evaluation, and criticism of issues in any part of their field.[10]

Dance writers have depended on conceptual and methodological models from other fields, especially from aesthetics. Theoretical models borrowed from other fields are automatically limited by their own paradigms, including research methods and basic yet often unstated assumptions and values. The use by dance scholars of theoretical constructs not derived from a dance research paradigm inadvertently precludes the consideration of parts of dance which do not fit the borrowed theory.

Among dance writers, except for Laban and his students such as Adshead, Hutchinson-Guest, and Bartenieff, constructing dance theory has taken precedence over finding adequate research methodology or articulating a dance-based paradigm for the field. In contrast, this book on dance-based dance theory presents both an inductively evolved research tool, the Framework of Topics Intrinsic to Dance Theory, to evaluate comprehensive dance theory, and a Model which defines the parameters and therefore articulates a paradigm for the field of dance. The Model incorporates all of the dimensions of dance that Adshead's methods cover and goes beyond them. The Model makes explicit a basic idea which until now, has remained implicit in theoretical writing about the field of dance: it integrates the historical, comparative, and systematic aspects of the field. Like Adshead's method, it offers a dance-based alternative to the practice of borrowing conceptual models from philosophy; the Model is based on dance practice and experience.

The Model, which has three parts, organizes the topics of the Framework which emerged from dance experience and from the writing of dance theorists and aestheticians. The *material, process,* and *work* are a functional unit in the Goal (G) of dance activity: to complete a dance work (fig. 2, next page).

G   *The Goal: A Dance*

W = Work
P = Process
M = Material

FIGURE 2. Components of *The Goal*

The *work*, choreographed and performed (*process*) by dancers (*material*) facilitates *Communication* (**C**) among participants and observers.

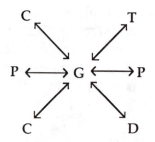

C *Communication*

T = Teacher
D = Dancer
P = Performance
W = Work
C = Choreographer

FIGURE 3. Interrelations of *Communication*

The Goal (**G**) and *Communication* (**C**) are seen and understood by people in several and distinct and at times overlapping roles, the *viewpoints* (fig. 4).

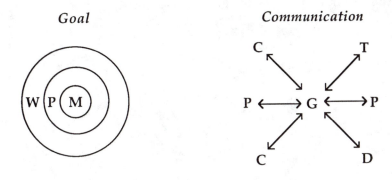

Goal   Communication

Viewpoints
Dancer   Teacher
Choreographer
Critic   Theorist
Scholar   Audience
Therapist

FIGURE 4. The Role of *Viewpoints*

The environment is the past and present *cultural context* (**CC**) in which the background, processes, and functions of dance (the *goal* and *communication*) are ongoing (fig. 5).

CC   *Cultural Context*

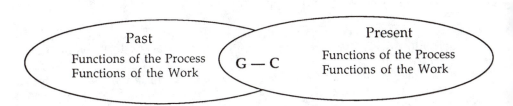

Past
Functions of the Process
Functions of the Work

G — C

Present
Functions of the Process
Functions of the Work

FIGURE 5. The Place of *Cultural Context*

The *synthesis* schematically shows interrelationships of the entire field of dance where the *goal* and *communication* are centered in the environment (fig. 6). The *work* is central and basic to the *goal*, the *communication*, the *cultural context*, and the *synthesis*.

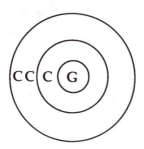

G = *The Goal*
C = *Communication*
CC = *Cultural Context*

FIGURE 6. The *Synthesis* of the Three Parts

Dance is a performing activity, and its product is seen in the process of performance. The notation of a dance provides a score which facilitates study, analysis, and theorizing about it because theoretical observations emanate from a specific dance and not just from the choreographer's, or critic's, or historian's, or ethnographer's, or audience member's ideas about it. When the dance itself is recognized as definitional and as separate from the dancer's performance and the choreographer's creative process (though related to both), then the complex unit of theory-practice can be understood as an ongoing seamless process of artistic and analytical exposition. The relationships among the features of any dance, all centered around the work itself, are embodied in the Model (fig. 7).

EXPLANATION OF THE MODEL: The *material, process*, and *work* combine in a functional unit in the *Goal* (G) of dance activity: to complete a dance. The work facilitates *Communication* (C) among several participants. G and C are seen and understood by people in several distinct and at times overlapping roles, listed in *viewpoints*. The *Cultural Context* (CC) is the past and present background, processes and functions of dance in which the *Goal* (G) and the *Communication* (C) are ongoing. The *Synthesis* schematically shows interrelationships of the entire field of dance where the goal and communication are centered in the cultural context. The *Work* is central and basic to G, C, CC, and the *Synthesis*.

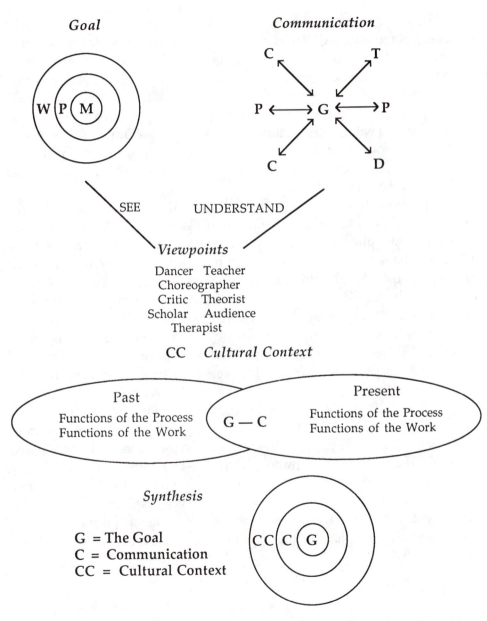

FIGURE 7. Diagram of a Model for Dance Theory

Research in dance is multi-focussed and interdisciplinary; it can be studied from many academic viewpoints. When studying dance as part of religious and cultural rituals, methods from anthropology are useful. When studying social dance as a form of courtship and a means of recreation, methods of sociology may be applicable. When studying dance-related injuries, data and therapies from sports medicine may be informative. When relevant, concepts and research methods from other fields can be tested for how accurately they apply to actual dance experience and not used like a cookie cutter into which some of the parts of dance are forced while the rest are left out.

This study began as an attempt to expose the problems caused by the traditional pattern found in the writing of many dance theorists who uncritically apply philosophic concepts, methods, and styles to their writing of comprehensive dance theory. The result of the study reveals much inadequate theoretical writing about dance stemming from incomplete research methods, borrowed concepts, and the prevalance of jargon in writing. Uncritical borrowing of theories and research methods leads to incomplete and inaccurate reporting about dance because the theoretical models of these disciplines emerge directly from their unique realms of knowledge, they use jargon geared to the field's specific activity; the theories, methods, and jargon may not apply entirely to dance.

Writings about dance by non-experts must not be confounded with either primary or secondary source material. Dance scholars must reorder their method of dance research by focussing on the dance and dance-based experience, (the primary source) and dance-based literature written by dance experts, (the secondary source) to develop methods of research, terminology, and theoretical constructs. In dance research, the initial step to study any part of dance must be the study of the actual physical, psychological, physiological, cultural, and mysterious experience of the dance itself.

NOTES

1 John Martin, *The Modern Dance* (1933; rpt. Brooklyn, N.Y.: Dance Horizons, 1965), 1.

2 Gertrude Lippincott, "A Dancer's Note to Aestheticians," *Journal of Aesthetics and Art Criticism*, 8 (1949), 103, 100.

3 Merce Cunningham, "The Impermanent Art," in *Esthetics Contemporary*, ed. Richard Kostelantz (Buffalo, N.Y.: Prometheus Books, 1978), 310.

4 George Beiswanger, "Rakes's Progress or Dances and the Critic," *Dance Scope*, 10:2 (Spring-Summer, 1976), 29, 30.

5 Maria Drabecka, "The Cinque Passi Step of the Galliard," *Dance Studies* 1(1976), 65-73.

6 Lucy Venable, "Labanotation" in "Movement Notation Systems" ed. Seymour Kleinman, *Quest Monograph*, 23 (Winter, 1975), 44-50.

7 Muriel Topaz, "Issues and Answers Concerning Reconstruction," *Choreography and Dance: The Notation Issue*, 1:1 (1988), 55-67.

8 Valerie Preston-Dunlop, ed., *Dancing and Dance Theory* (London: Laban Art of Movement Centre, 1979).

9 Janet Adshead, *The Study of Dance* (London: Dance Books Ltd., 1981); Janet Adshead, Pauline Hodgens, Valerie A. Briginshaw, and Michael Huxley, *Dance Analysis: Theory and Practice*, ed. Janet Adshead, (London: Dance Books, 1988), 4.

10 Thomas S. Kuhn, *The Structure of Scientific Revolutions*, 2nd ed., enlarged (Chicago: University of Chicago Press, 1970).

BIBLIOGRAPHY

Adshead, Janet. *The Study of Dance*. London: Dance Books Ltd., 1981.

Adshead, Janet, Valerie A. Briginshaw, Pauline Hodgens, and Michael Huxley. *Dance Analysis: Theory and Practice*. Ed. Janet Adshead. London: Dance Books, 1988.

Alter, Judith B. "A Critical Analysis of Susanne K. Langer's Dance Theory." In *A Spectrum of World Dance*, Dance Research Annual 16, ed. L. A. Wallen and Joan Acocella, 110-119. New York: Congress on Research in Dance, 1987.

_____. Concert Notebook: *Facade* by Edith Sitwell and William Walton. Thesis Mills College, 1970.

_____. "Music and Rhythm in Dance: H'Doubler's Views in Retrospect." In *Conference Proceedings, 1984* of The Society for Dance History Scholars. Riverside, Calif.: University of California, Riverside, Dance Department, 1984.

_____. "Sleuthing Havelock Ellis's Essay 'The Art of Dance.'" In *Conference Proceedings, 1985* of The Society for Dance History Scholars. Riverside, Calif.: University of California, Riverside, Dance Department, 1985.

Armelagos, Adina, and Mary Sirridge. "The Identity Crisis in Dance." *Journal of Aesthetics and Art Criticism*, 37 (1978), 129-139.

Ayer, Alfred Jules. *Language, Truth, and Logic*. 1936; rpt. New York: Dover Publications, 1952.

Bartenieff, Irmgard. "The Roots of Laban Theory: Aesthetics and Beyond." In *Four Adaptations of Effort Shape Theory in Research and Teaching*, ed. I. M. Bartenieff, M. Davis, and F. Pauley, 1-28. New York: Dance Notation Bureau, 1970.

Beardsley, Monroe C. *Aesthetics from Classical Greece to the Present: A Short History*. New York: Macmillan, 1966.

Beck, Jill. "Labanotation: Implications for the Future of Dance." In *Choreography and Dance: The Notation Issue*, ed. Muriel Topaz, 1:1 (1988), 69-91.

Beiswanger, George. "Doing and Viewing Dances: A Perspective for the Practice of Criticism." *Dance Perspectives*, 55 (1973), 7-13.

_____. "Rake's Progress or Dances and the Critic." *Dance Scope*, 10:2 (Spring-Summer 1976), 29-33.

Bell, Clive. *Art*. London: Chatto and Windus, 1914.

Benthall, Jonathan and Ted Polhemus. *Body as Medium of Expression*. London: Allen Lane, 1975.

Best, David. *Expression in Movement and the Arts*. London: Lepus Books, 1974.

_____. *Philosophy and Human Movement*. London: George Allen and Unwin, 1978.

Blasis, Carlo. *Traité Élémentaire, Théorique et Pratique de l'Art de la Danse*. Milan: Beauti et Tementi, 1820. Trans. by Mary Stewart Evans under the title *An Elementary Treatise upon the Theory and Practice of the Art of Dancing*. New York: Dover Publications, 1968.

Bullough, Edward. "'Psychical Distance' as a Factor in Art and an Aesthetic Principle." *British Journal of Psychology*, 5:2 (1912), 87-118.

Cahusac, Louis de. *La Danse Ancienne et Moderne*. 3 vol. La Haye: J. Neaulime, 1754.

Carter, Curtis. "Some Notes on Aesthetics and Dance Criticism." *Dance Scope*, 10:2 (Spring-Summer 1976), 35-39.

Cohen, Selma Jeanne. "A Prolegomenon to an Aesthetics of Dance." *Journal of Aesthetics and Art Criticism*, 21 (1962), 19-26.

_____. *Next Week, Swan Lake*. Middletown, Conn.: Wesleyan University Press, 1982.

_____. "Some Theories of Dance in Contemporary Society." *Journal of Aesthetics and Art Criticism*, 9 (1950), 111-118.

Collingwood, R. G. *The Principles of Art*. 1938; rpt. London: Oxford University Press, 1974.

Courtney, Richard. "On Langer's Dramatic Illusion." *Journal of Aesthetics and Art Criticism*, 29 (1970), 11-20.

Cunningham, Merce. "The Impermanent Art." In *Esthetics Contemporary*, ed. Richard Kostelantz, 310-314. Buffalo, N.Y.: Prometheus Books, 1978.

Dewey, John. *Art as Experience*. 1934; rpt. New York: Putnam's Capricorn Books, 1958.

Dickie, George. *Art and the Aesthetic*. Ithaca, N.Y.: Cornell University Press, 1974.

_____. "Bullough and the Concept of Psychical Distance." *Philosophy and Phenomenological Research* 22: 2 (1961), 33-38.

Drabecka, Maria. "A Comparative Study of the *Cinque Passi* —A Basic Step of the Galliard." *Dance Studies* 1 (1976) 65-73.

Ellis, Havelock. *The Dance of Life*. Boston: Houghton-Mifflin, 1923.

Feibleman, James K. *Aesthetics: A Study of the Fine Arts in Theory and Practice*. New York: Duell, Sloan and Pearce, 1949.

Flaccus, Louis W. *The Spirit and Substance of Art*. New York: F. S. Crofts, 1941.

Foster, John. *The Influence of Rudolf Laban*. London: Lepus Books, 1978.

Foster, Susan L. *Reading Dancing: Bodies and Subjects in Contemporary American Dance*. Berkeley and Los Angeles: University of California Press, 1986.

Fraleigh, Sondra. *Dance and the Lived Body: A Descriptive Aesthetics*. Pittsburgh: University of Pittsburgh Press, 1988.

Friedman, James Michael. *Dancer and Spectator: An Aesthetic Distance.* San Francisco: Ballet Monographs, 1976.

_____. *The Dancer and Other Aesthetic Objects.* San Francisco: Ballet Monographs, 1980.

Gilbert, K. A. and Helmut Kuhn. *A History of Esthetics.* Bloomington, Ind.: Indiana University Press, 1953.

Gilson, Etienne. *Forms and Substance of the Arts.* New York: Scribner's Sons, 1966.

Goodman, Nelson. *Languages of Art.* Indianapolis: Hackett Publishing Company, 1976.

Gray, Judith Anne. "To Want To Dance: A Biography of Margaret H'Doubler." Diss. University of Arizona, 1978.

Greene, Theodore Meyer. *The Arts and Art Criticism.* Princeton: Princeton University Press, 1940.

Hackney, Peggy, Sarah Manno, and Muriel Topaz. *Study Guide for Elementary Labanotation.* New York: Dance Notation Bureau Press, 1977.

Hanna, Judith Lynne. *To Dance Is Human: A Theory of Nonverbal Communication.* Austin: University of Texas Press, 1979.

Hawkins, Alma, "A Look at the Future." In *Dance: A Projection for the Future,* ed. Marian Van Tuyl, 97-111. San Francisco: Impulse Publications, Inc., 1968.

H'Doubler, Margaret, *A Manual of Dancing.* Madison, Wis.: published by the author, 1921.

_____. *Dance: A Creative Art Experience.* 1940; Madison, Wis.: University of Wisconsin Press, 1959.

_____. *The Dance and Its Place in Education.* New York: Harcourt Brace and Co., 1925.

Hirn, Yrjo. *The Origins of Art: A Psychological and Sociological Inquiry.* New York: The Macmillan Co., 1900.

Howard, Vernon A. "Music and Constant Comment." *Erkenntnis,* 12 (1978), 73-82.

_____. "On Musical Expression." *British Journal of Aesthetics,* 11 (1971), 268-280.

Hutchinson-Guest, Ann. *Dance Notation: The Process of Recording Movement on Paper.* New York: Dance Horizons, 1984.

Kaelin, Eugene R. *Art and Existence: A Phenomenological Aesthetic.* Lewisburg, Pa.: Bucknell University Press, 1970.

Kainz, Friedrich. *Vorlesungen ueber Aesthetik.* Wien: Sexl-Verlag, 1948. Trans. by Herbert M. Schueller under the title *Aesthetics: The Science.* Detroit: Wayne State University Press, 1962.

Kaprelian, Mary. H. *Aesthetics for Dancers: A Selected Annotated Bibliography.* Washington: AAHPER Publications, 1976.

Khatchadourian, Haig. "The Expression Theory of Art: A Critical Evaluation." *Journal of Aesthetics and Art Criticism,* 23 (1965), 335-352.

Kuhn, Thomas S. *The Structure of Scientific Revolutions.* 2nd ed., enlarged. Chicago: University of Chicago Press, 1970.

Laban, Rudolf. "The Aesthetic Approach to the Art of Dancing." *LAMGM,* 23 (1959), 29-32.

_____. *A Life for Dance.* New York: Theatre Arts Books, 1975.

_____. "The Art of Movement in the School." *LAMGM,* 9 (1952), 10-16.

_____. "Dance and Symbol." *Laban Art of Movement Guild Magazine* [*LAMGM*], 22 (1959), 25-28.

_____. "Education Through the Arts." *LAMGM,* 19 (1957). In *Rudolf Laban Speaks about Movement and Dance* [*RLSMD*], ed. Lisa Ullman, 3-6. London: Laban Art of Movement Centre, 1971. .

_____. "Extract from an Address held by Mr. Laban on a Meeting for Community-Dance in 1936." *LAMGM*, 52 (1974), 6-11.

_____. "The Importance of Dancing." *LAMGM*, 22 (1959). *RLSMD*, 11-21.

_____. "Laban Lecture." *LAMGM*, 12 (1954), 22-25.

_____. "Laban Lecture, 1957: Movement: An Art and a Philosophy." *LAMGM*, 18 (1957), 6-13.

_____. *The Mastery of Movement*. London: Macdonald and Evans, 1960.

_____. "Meaning." *LAMGM*, 22 (1959), 29-31.

_____. *Modern Educational Dance*. London: Macdonald and Evans, 1948.

_____. "The Rhythm of Effort and Recovery, Part II." *LAMGM*, 24 (1960), 13-18.

_____. "The Rhythm of Living Energy." *LAMGM*, 22 (1959), 40-47.

_____. "The Three R's of the Art of Movement Practice: Recreation, Research, Rehabilitation." *LAMGM*, 14 (1955), 12-17.

_____. "What Has Led You to Study Movement?" *LAMGM*, 7 (1952), 7-10.

_____. *Choreutics*. Ed. Lisa Ullman. London: Macdonald and Evans, 1966.

Laban, Rudolf and Lawrence, F. C. *Effort*. London: Macdonald and Evans, 1947.

Langer, Susanne K. *Feeling and Form: A Theory Developed from Philosophy in a New Key*. New York: Scribner's Sons, 1953.

_____. *Philosophy in a New Key: A Study in the Symbolism of Reason, Rite, and Art*. Cambridge, Mass.: Harvard University Press, 1942.

_____. *Problems of Art*. New York: Scribner's Sons, 1957.

_____. *Mind: An Essay on Human Feeling*. Baltimore: Johns Hopkins University Press, 1982.

Lee, Harry B. "The Cultural Lag in Aesthetics." *Journal of Aesthetics and Art Criticism*, 6 (1947), 120-131.

Lippincott, Gertrude. "A Dancer's Note to Aestheticians." *Journal of Aesthetics and Art Criticism*, 8 (1949), 97-105.

Lipps, Theodor. *Psychological Studies*. Tr. Herbert S. Sanborn. Baltimore: Williams and Wilkins, Co., 1926.

Lorber, Richard. "Editorial: The Coming of Age of Dance Criticism." *Dance Scope*, 10:1 (1975-1976), 9-10.

Maletic, Vera. *Body—Space—Expression: The Development of Rudolf Laban's Movement and Dance Concepts*. Berlin: Mouton de Gruyter, 1987.

Margolis, Joseph, ed. *Philosophy Looks at the Arts*. Philadelphia: Temple University Press, 1978.

Martin, John. *America Dancing*. New York: Dodge Publishers, 1936.

_____. *Introduction to the Dance*. New York: W. W. Norton, 1939; rpt. Brooklyn, N.Y.: Dance Horizons Press, 1965.

_____. *The Modern Dance*. New York: A. S. Barnes, 1933; rpt. Brooklyn, N.Y.: Dance Horizons Press, 1965.

_____. *The Dance: The Story of the Dance Told in Pictures and Text*. New York: Tudor Publishing Company, 1946.

Metheny, Eleanor. *Movement and Meaning*. New York: McGraw-Hill, 1968.

Munro, Thomas. *The Arts and Their Interrelations*. New York: The Liberal Arts Press, 1949.

_____. "'The Afternoon of a Faun' and the Interrelation of the Arts." *Journal of Aesthetics and Art Criticism*, 10 (1951), 95-109.

Nagel, Ernest. Review of *Philosophy in a New Key*, by S. K. Langer. *Journal of Philosophy*, 40 (1943), 323-329.

Norton, Richard. "What is Virtuality?" *Journal of Aesthetics and Art Criticism*, 30 (1972), 499-505.

Noverre, Jean Georges. *Lettres sur la Danse et les Ballets*. A. Lyon: Chez Aime Delaroche, Imprimeur-libraire du Gouvernement et de la Ville, aux Halles, 1783). Tr. of 1930 edition by Cyril W. Beaumont under the title *Letters on Dancing and Ballets*; rpt., Brooklyn, N.Y.: Dance Horizons, 1966.

Osborne, Harold. *Aesthetics and Art Theory: An Historical Introduction*. New York: E.P. Dutton, 1970.

Parker, DeWitt. *The Principles of Aesthetics*. Boston: Silver, Burdett, 1920.

Passmore, John A. *A Hundred Years of Philosophy*. New York: Basic Books, 1966.

Phenix, Philip H. *Realms of Meaning: A Philosophy of the Curriculum for General Education*. New York: McGraw-Hill, 1964.

Polhemus, Ted, ed. *The Body Reader: Special Aspects of the Human Body*. New York: Pantheon Books, 1978.

Preston-Dunlop, Valerie, ed., *Dancing and Dance Theory*. London: Laban Art of Movement Centre, 1979.

Prevots, Naima. *American Pageantry: A Movement for Art and Democracy*. Ann Arbor, Mich: UMI Research Press, 1990.

Reid, Louis Arnaud. "Feeling and Expression in the Arts: Expression, Sense and Feelings." *Journal of Aesthetics and Art Criticism*, 25, (1966), 123-135.

_____. "Susanne Langer and Beyond." *British Journal of Aesthetics*, 5 (1965), 357-367.

Reiser, Max. "The Semantic Theory of Art in America." *Journal of Aesthetics and Art Criticism*, 15 (1956), 12-26.

Ross, Malcolm. *The Aesthetic Impulse*. Oxford: Pergamon Press, 1981.

Rudner, Richard. "On Semiotic Aesthetics." *Journal of Aesthetics and Art Criticism*, 10 (1951), 67-77.

Sachs, Curt. *World History of the Dance*. New York: W. W. Norton, 1937.

Selden, Elizabeth. *Elements of the Free Dance*. New York: A. S. Barnes, 1930.

_____. *The Dancer's Quest*. Berkeley: University of California Press, 1935.

Sheets-Johnstone, Maxine. *The Phenomenology of Dance*. Madison, Wis.: University of Wisconsin Press, 1966.

Sircello, Guy. *Mind and Art: An Essay on the Varieties of Expression*. Princeton: Princeton University Press, 1972.

Sirridge, Mary, and Adina Armelagos. "The In's and Out's of Dance: Expression as an Aspect of Style." *Journal of Aesthetics and Art Criticism*, 37 (1978), 16-24.

Sorell, Walter. "The Literaté Dancer." *Dance Scope*, 10:2 (Spring-Summer 1976), 40-44.

Sparshott, Francis. *Off the Ground: First Steps to a Philosophical Consideration of Dance*. Princeton: Princeton University Press, 1988.

Stodelle, Ernestine. "A Dancer's Philosopher: Susanne K. Langer." *Dance Observer*, 30 (1963), 69-70.

Szathmary, Arthur. "Symbolic and Aesthetic Expression in Painting." *Journal of Aesthetics and Art Criticism*, 13 (1954), 86-96.

Thornton, Samuel. *Laban's Theory of Movement: A New Perspective*. Boston: Plays, Inc., 1971.

Topaz, Muriel. "Issues and Answers Concerning Reconstruction." *Choreography and Dance: The Notation Issue*, 1:1 (1988), 55-67.

Torossian, Aram. *A Guide to Aesthetics*. Palo Alto, Calif.: Stanford University Press, 1927.

Venable, Lucy. "Labanotation." In "Movement Notation Systems," ed. Seymour Kleinman. *Quest Monograph,* 23 (Winter 1975), 44-50.

Weaver, John. *An Essay Towards an History of Dancing.* London: J. Tomson, 1712.

Weiss, Paul. *Nine Basic Arts.* Carbondale, Ill.: Southern Illinois University Press, 1961.

Weitz, Morris. *Philosophy of the Arts.* New York: Russell & Russell, 1950.

_____. "Symbolism and Art." *Review of Metaphysics,* 7 (1954), 466-481.

Winnicott, D. W. *Playing and Reality.* London: Penguin Books, 1982.

Youngerman, Suzanne. "Curt Sachs and His Heritage: A Critical Review of *World History of the Dance* with a Survey of Recent Studies That Perpetuate His Ideas." *CORD News,* 1-2 (1974), 6-19.

_____. "Movement Notation Systems as Conceptual Frameworks: The Laban System." In *Illuminating Dance: Philosophical Explorations.* Ed. Maxine Sheets-Johnstone. Lewisburg, Pa: Bucknell University Press, 1984.

Zimmerman, Robert L. "Can Anything Be an Aesthetic Object?" *Journal of Aesthetics and Art Criticism,* 25 (1966), 177-186.

INDEX

A

abstraction, 23, 36, 38, 62, 72, 87, 91, 119, 124, 169–170
Adshead, Janet, 170, 171
aesthetic experience, 13, 72
aesthetic intention (goal), 14, 15, 59–60, 73, 74, 125, 132, 152
aesthetic result (effect), 14, 15, 60, 125, 132, 147
aesthetics, 2, 4, 5, 105, 171
aestheticians, 2, 3, 5, 6-7, 62, 78, 97, 105–126, 129, 131, 134, 136, 142
anatomy, 76
anthropology, 1, 17, 18, 142, 157, 176
anti-ballet idea. *See* ballet
architecture, 71, 91
Armitage, Merle, 39
Art, 17, 28, 47, 75, 122
arts, other than dance, 13, 24, 29, 38, 57, 58, 60, 61, 71, 72, 91, 94, 158
audience, 13, 15, 17, 25, 26, 27, 34, 38, 47, 58, 59, 60, 66, 69, 73, 74, 85, 91, 122, 132–133, 145, 149, 152
autonomous field, dance as, 1, 8, 56, 57, 97

B

ballet, 1, 4, 7, 40, 48, 50, 53, 54, 56, 57, 59, 61, 68, 69, 75, 86, 99, 113, 114, 124
ballroom as dance space, 115
ballroom dance. *See* social dance
Bartenieff, Irmgard, 33, 36, 38, 171
Beiswanger, George, 132, 164–165
Bell, Clive, 87
Best, David, 125
Blasis, Carlo, 3
body, 23, 38, 48, 50, 52, 57, 66–67, 68, 72, 74, 84, 109, 130, 144–145, 156

C

Cahusac, Louis de, 3
"center" defined, 4, 50, 51
choreographer, creator, inventor, 14, 15, 18, 51, 59, 68, 147, 166